Grills gone Vegan

Tamasin Noyes

Book Publishing Company
Summertown, Tennessee

Cover and interior design: Deirdre Nemmers
Lead food stylist: Ron Maxen
Assistant food stylists: Barbara Jefferson and Liz Murray
Photography: Andrew Schmidt

Calculations for the nutritional analyses in this book are based on the average number of servings listed with the recipes and the average amount of an ingredient if a range is called for. Calculations are rounded up to the nearest gram. If two options for an ingredient are listed, the first one is used. Not included are optional ingredients and serving suggestions.

Book Publishing Company
PO Box 99, Summertown, TN 38483
888-260-8458 ● bookpubco.com

ISBN 13: 978-1-57067-290-3

19 18 17 16 15 14 13   1 2 3 4 5 6 7 8 9

Printed in Canada

Library of Congress Cataloging-in-Publication Data
Noyes, Tamasin.
Grills gone vegan / Tamasin Noyes.
pages cm
Includes index.
ISBN 978-1-57067-290-3 (pbk.) -- ISBN 978-1-57067-909-4 (e-book)
1. Vegan cooking. 2. Barbecuing. I. Title.
TX837.N695 2013
641.5'636--dc23
2012038462

Book Publishing Company is a member of Green Press Initiative. We chose to print this title on paper with 100% postconsumer recycled content, processed without chlorine, which saved the following natural resources:

- 49 trees
- 1,528 pounds of solid waste
- 22, 824 gallons of water
- 4,209 pounds of greenhouse gases
- 22 million BTU of energy

For more information on Green Press Initiative, visit www.greenpressinitiative.org. Environmental impact estimates were made using the Environmental Defense Fund Paper Calculator. For more information visit www.papercalculator.org.

CONTENTS

For Jim, Kevin, and my family—past, present, and always.

ACKNOWLEDGMENTS

Even though only the author's name appears on the cover, books are truly a group effort. After I develop my recipes, an incredible team of testers scrutinizes each one. Many thanks to this terrific group of people, who tirelessly and enthusiastically shared their kitchens, time, and valuable input: Liz Wyman, Elaine Trautwein, Celine Steen, Thalia Palmer, Celia Ozerko, Amy Mekemson, Clea Mahoney, Jenn Lynskey, Kim Lahn, Aimee Kluiber, Kim Eads, Kip Dorrell, Shannon Davis, Kayla Clough, Kelly Cavalier, and Vegan Aide.

Then it's on to the wonderful people at Book Publishing Company, who put so much thoughtful energy into producing the finished book that you hold in your hands. Thank you to Bob and Cynthia Holzapfel for their belief in this project, to Jo Stepaniak for her endless patience and invaluable experience, and to Jasmine Star and Deirdre Nemmers for their talents in pulling this book together.

I'd also like to thank you—yes, you! Whether you're vegan or aspiring to be (even for just an occasional meal), thank you not only for purchasing this book, but for bringing veganism into your life.

Finally, a big thank-you to everyone in the amazing vegan community. From the committed business owners to the vegan cookbook authors who came before me (and those who will come after) to the vegan bloggers to the people I meet in the grocery store, thank you for sharing my ideals and being the inspiration that you are!

INTRODUCTION

Whether you are cooking for just a few people or for many, no style of cooking lends itself to easy, casual, and interactive entertaining the way grilling does. Vegan grilling is becoming more mainstream as cooks realize the potential it offers for getting big flavors from food. Plus, people tend to gather around fires and food, so putting the two together creates social magic. Cooking over a flame has been in our genes for centuries, but the recent shift toward a more healthful style of eating calls for new recipes and techniques.

Cooking indoors using a grill pan on the stove or an electric grill (which may serve double duty as a griddle, panini press, or waffle iron) offers incredible versatility when it comes to getting those great grill flavors year-round. As a result, we are no longer limited by the season or weather, or bound to outdoor grilling on charcoal or gas grills. While these types of grills have their place and are traditional, not everyone has access to an outdoor grill or the desire to use one. An indoor grill, on the other hand, offers kitchen convenience, along with options for using it in new and interesting ways. As a result, grilling—and vegan grilling in particular—has evolved into far more than kabobs on skewers.

One of the greatest advantages of grill-style cooking is the flexibility it brings. Is the kitchen too hot to even consider turning on the stove? Head to the patio or deck. Is it pouring rain outside? Shift the plan from an outdoor grill to a grill pan. Is there a power outage? Fire up that gas or charcoal grill. Once you've read chapter 1, which is full of grilling techniques and tips, improvising for any occasion will be easy.

Chapter 2, Scrumptious Starters and Small Plates, is sure to please the palate. There's something for everyone in this chapter, and many of these recipes can also be served as side dishes.

Chapter 3, Sensational Soups and Sandwiches, offers recipes that span the planet—some with exotic flavors, and others that are American classics. Red Bell Pepper Gazpacho (page 48) pairs beautifully with BBQ Portobello Grillers (page 72). Chimichurri Wraps (page 52) and The Veg Wedge (page 56) are as different (and tasty!) as can be. Feature a few of your favorite sandwiches for a casual party and watch the food disappear. Keep in mind that the marinades used for some of the sandwiches work well in other applications, so be creative with them.

In the heat of the day, you'll be thrilled to have the option of cooking the main dishes in chapter 4 outdoors. Or adapt these recipes for indoor cooking to warm your kitchen in the winter. Hearty Tempeh-Chickpea Stew with Harissa Biscuits (page 116) and Porcini and Sausage Paella (page 118) are sure to impress guests—or your family. How about a calzone on the grill? You bet! The Broccoli and Cheeze Calzones (page 112) will rival the fare at your favorite pizzeria.

For that space on the plate next to the main dish, see chapter 5, Super Side Dishes. Extra-easy Garlicky Cauliflower (page 131), Smoky Packet Potatoes (page 135), and Lemony Greek Barley Salad (page 128) are crowd-pleasers. Don't miss the Asian Sesame Noodles (page 138), a less oily version of the take-out classic.

Turning to chapter 6, indulge in tantalizing grilled desserts, whether you are cooking inside or out. Almost-Instant Apple Pies with Dark Caramel Sauce (page 149) come together in just minutes. Skillet-Grilled Mango-Blueberry Cobbler (page 147), with its tropical twist on a traditional recipe, is both comforting and contemporary. For an elegant finish, try the Peach Melba (page 144).

Chapter 7, Remarkable Rubs, Marinades, and Sauces, includes a variety of seasonings and condiments that can be mixed and matched with your choice of proteins or vegetables. These handy recipes, such as All-Purpose Dry Rub (page 158) and Red-Hot Chimichurri Sauce (page 168), can be used in many ways. Smoke Booster (page 161) is a versatile concoction that brings a flavorful lower note to many of these recipes. Keep some on hand for instant flavor.

Every recipe in this book offers indoor cooking options, so you can put together a satisfying and delectable grill meal in any weather or season, and with any type of grilling equipment. To help you get started, see the suggested menus in Grilling for Any Occasion (page 17).

Whether you're aiming for a casual family meal or an impressive feast for guests, this guide to vegan grilling will help you make the most of every occasion. With these recipes on the outdoor grill, your backyard may become the neighborhood gathering place. In winter the party may just move indoors as you continue your grilling endeavors in the kitchen. If there is anything in life more satisfying than nurturing others through cooking, I haven't found it. In that spirit, allow me to share *Grills Gone Vegan* with you. Happy grilling!

Chapter 1
Getting Started

Buying an Outdoor Grill

Before you purchase an outdoor grill, think about your style and preferences. Do you have the patience and flexibility for charcoal grilling, or would you prefer a gas grill for convenient weeknight grilling? Or maybe traditional low-tech cooking over a campfire appeals to you. If that's the case, keep in mind that many of the recipes in this book can also be prepared over an open fire.

Gas Grills

Using a gas grill is probably the easiest method of outdoor grilling. Thanks to a propane tank, it's only a matter of turning a few knobs, and you'll be cooking with fire—literally. As an added bonus, gas grills are quick to heat up (just preheat for ten minutes) and easy to clean. On the downside, some die-hard grillers feel gas grills don't create authentic grill flavors and prefer charcoal or wood for the heat source. If you choose to use a gas grill, however, you can compensate by using the techniques in the section Maximizing Grill Flavors (page 8).

If a gas grill doesn't have individual burner controls, the entire grill will heat to one temperature. Multiple burners are a better option, offering more control and allowing the cook to use hotter or cooler sections of the grill as needed. Another feature to keep in mind is the size of the grill surface. Chances are you'll want a lot of space, and it can be a hassle to need more space than you have.

Gas grills can be expensive, but with proper care they will last for years. As with all technology, the cost of high-end features is coming down as they become more widely available. One very convenient feature showing up in more reasonably priced grills is a built-in thermometer. However, if your grill, or the grill of your dreams, doesn't have one, no problem. An oven thermometer can be used instead.

To be ready to grill at a moment's notice, always keep an extra propane tank on hand. Be sure the propane tank is securely and safely hooked up and that there is no gas smell, which might indicate a leak. Preheat the grill for about ten minutes before cooking. When you're finished cooking, turn off the burners and propane tank. It's easiest to clean the grill grates while they're still warm. Follow the manufacturer's instructions for cleaning.

Charcoal Grills

A distinct advantage of charcoal grills is that they are portable, making them ideal for on-the-go lifestyles. It takes a little practice to get the charcoal burning, and sometimes it takes longer than you'd like for the fire to get hot enough for cooking. On the upside, there's something to be said for the ritual of fire building, as long as time isn't an issue. Plus, by arranging the charcoal, it's easy to create hotter spots on the grill. As a rule, charcoal grills are less expensive than gas grills.

Plan ahead so the grill will be hot enough for cooking at the right time. Fire needs air, so open the vents of the grill. A chimney starter (discussed later in this chapter) is the easiest way to get a charcoal grill going quickly. Follow the instructions for the chimney starter, dumping the starter coals into the grill when they're coated with a thin layer of ash. Spread the starter coals in the grill and then add the cooking charcoal, spreading it evenly too. It may take twenty to thirty minutes for the chimney starter and coals to be ready for cooking, so it's important to plan ahead.

The top vent is used to control the temperature, while the bottom vent should be left open to allow air to feed the fire. When you're done cooking, let the embers cool completely before removing them to an ash can (it's essential to have an ash can to safely dispose of the ashes).

Buying an Indoor Grill

If your budget and storage space permit, you might eventually want to have all three indoor grill options: a cast-iron grill pan, a nonstick grill pan, and an electric grill. It's easy to find uses for all three. If you opt for just one, an electric grill, while the most expensive, is also the most versatile. Electric grills are often on sale at big box stores.

Grill Pans

There are two kinds of grill pans: cast-iron and nonstick. Cast-iron grill pans, when properly seasoned, are virtually nonstick. They can also be heavy. These are ideal for making grilled flatbreads, pizzas, and panini indoors. One popular brand of cast-iron cookware offers a reversible grill pan with a smooth side in addition to the ridged side. While that versatility may seem tempting, once the smooth side is seasoned, it can't be placed against a stove burner.

Nonstick grill pans give bold grilling marks. Just be aware that even though they are nonstick, cleaning the valleys between the ridges can be challenging.

When using a grill pan on the stove, it's natural for it to smoke. That's part of what gives the food authentic grill flavor, but it can

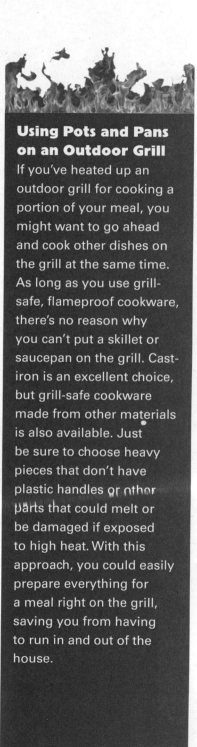

Using Pots and Pans on an Outdoor Grill
If you've heated up an outdoor grill for cooking a portion of your meal, you might want to go ahead and cook other dishes on the grill at the same time. As long as you use grill-safe, flameproof cookware, there's no reason why you can't put a skillet or saucepan on the grill. Cast-iron is an excellent choice, but grill-safe cookware made from other materials is also available. Just be sure to choose heavy pieces that don't have plastic handles or other parts that could melt or be damaged if exposed to high heat. With this approach, you could easily prepare everything for a meal right on the grill, saving you from having to run in and out of the house.

also set off smoke detectors. Thankfully, in this case, where there's smoke, there isn't fire.

Electric Grills

Also called grillers or griddles, electric grills often have interchangeable plates, which offer tremendous flexibility. Some electric grills have three different plates: smooth plates, which are ideal for pancakes or toasted sandwiches; ridged plates, which are wonderful for everything else and are used in this book unless otherwise stated; and waffle plates. For even more options, some brands can be opened flat to give a large, open grilling surface with either smooth or ridged plates or both.

The interchangeable plates eliminate the need for extra appliances and are easy to clean. However, they do take up cabinet space. In most situations, it's best to cook with electric grills open, to mimic a grill pan. When they're closed, moist foods tend to steam more than grill. When the grill is open, cooking may take slightly longer, but the end results are worth it. Read Maximizing Grill Flavors (page 8) for helpful techniques for getting the best results from an electric grill.

For certain foods, however, such as sandwiches, it's best to cook with the grill closed (this is indicated in the recipes in this book). For the most even cooking, it's important to keep the grill plates flat and level. Sometimes the thickness of the food causes the lid to rise in the front. When this happens, the plates can't make full contact with the food. To counteract this, use a wooden spoon to slightly raise the top plate near the back of the grill to better level the plates.

Essential Utensils

For indoor grilling, your kitchen is probably already adequately equipped. For outdoor grilling, several standard tools are needed. A quick perusal of the grilling aisle at your favorite hardware or home store will be eye-opening. The number of new and unique grilling tools seems to grow daily. Although some are worthwhile, many others aren't practical or necessary for vegan cooking. Start with the basics and build your collection as your grilling experience grows.

Ash can. A metal ash can is vital for disposing ashes when using a charcoal grill. Be sure the charcoal is completely burnt out before transferring the ashes, and keep the can covered and away from other flammable items in case it heats up or sparks. For added safety, douse the ashes with water before disposal.

Assorted jars with lids. We all save little jars, don't we? Lidded jars are perfect for batches of marinade, but plastic containers or even small bowls also work well. The benefit of a jar is being able to grab a marinade from the refrigerator, shake it, and go. It's also a good way to reuse, rather than simply recycle, which is always a plus.

Basting brushes. To get every last bit of flavor from a marinade, brush the leftovers on the food as it cooks using a silicon basting brush. Silicon brushes can withstand very high temperatures and can be washed in a dishwasher. A long handle is preferable, to keep your hands and arms further from the heat of the grill.

Chimney starter. As mentioned, a chimney starter is the easiest way to jump-start a charcoal grill. Charcoal is confined to a can and heats to the point where it is coated with a layer of ash more quickly than if it is simply started in the grill. Refer to the instructions that come with the starter for the best results.

Foil roasting pans. Keep several different sizes of foil pans on hand. Recipes that require stirring, such as Grilled Ratatouille (page 132) and Cowboy Spaghetti (page 106) are much easier to make in these pans. If you take food to cook on somebody else's grill, using a foil pan ensures that the food won't touch any possible meat residue on the grill surface. If the pans are treated gently, they can be reused several times.

Grill sheet. When cooking foods that might fall between the grates of an outdoor grill, a grill sheet comes in handy. This is a large metal sheet perforated with many holes to allow cooking while preventing smaller food items from falling through. A grill sheet can also be used to create a barrier between the food and a questionable grill surface that may have been used to cook meat.

Heavy-duty baking mitt. Just like you wouldn't grab a hot pot without using pot holders, don't reach over the grill without using a baking mitt. Wear it like you mean business.

Nonreactive cookware. Nonreactive cookware refers to cookware that won't react with acids and is made of glass, ceramic, or stainless steel, or is enamel-coated.

Skewers. Both wooden and metal skewers are available. If using wooden skewers, be sure to soak them in water for at least thirty minutes before putting them on the grill. Metal skewers are reusable and come in straight sticks, swirls, or even bendable shapes. When using metal skewers, lightly oil or mist them with cooking spray so the food will slide off more easily.

Smoker box. A smoker box is a small metal container that can be used under the grill grates of a gas grill to impart a smoky flavor to foods. If using a gas grill, don't be caught without a smoker box, or try your hand at making the homemade foil packets described on page 11. While these aren't essential, the smoke they create goes a long way in creating flavor.

Spray bottle. A spray bottle isn't necessary, but it is handy to have. Fill the bottle with juice, wine, beer, or broth to spritz food while cooking for yet another layer of flavor.

Stovetop smoker. A stovetop smoker is a covered metal pan that can be used on the stove or a grill. Wood chips are spread in the bottom, and food is placed on a rack above the chips so the smoke from the chips can surround it. A stovetop smoker can be used for proteins or vegetables. Plus, it's just plain fun for experimenting with.

Thermometer. It might come as a surprise that a standard oven thermometer can be used right on the grill. However, it isn't necessary to have a thermometer on the grill. When using a gas grill, the burner knobs make it easy to target a temperature range. In fact, the recipes in this book specify heat level rather than specific temperatures.

Tongs and turners. You probably already have tongs and turners in your kitchen. But for grilling you'll want tools with long handles so you won't have to reach over the grill. Tongs get a lot of use in oiling the grill (as described later in this chapter) and are handy for moving vegetables around. A turner allows you to carefully lift food from the grill while preserving the grill marks.

Maximizing Grill Flavors

There's just something about the smoky flavor of foods cooked on a charcoal grill that's irresistible. To maximize that wonderful flavor, especially if using an electric grill, don't be afraid to adapt the recipe. Adding smoked paprika or liquid smoke or substituting smoked salt for regular salt will enhance the smoky flavor. Another option is to add little Smoke Booster (page 161) to a marinade or use it for basting. Keep in mind that seasonings and marinades can change in character when heated. For example, smoked paprika has more flavor once it's heated. The flavors of ingredients such as vinegar or wine tend to intensify. When adding spices, remember the old adage that you can add flavor, but you can't take it out, so start with a small amount and add more to taste.

Flavor can be added to grilled foods at many points along the way. Use the methods discussed in this section as you wish, and consider combining two or more of these options for bigger, bolder taste.

Marinating is your first opportunity to create a grilled masterpiece, infusing flavor into the food. After marinating, try a spice rub to add flavor to the surface. When grilling, use a smoker box or improvise one with a foil packet for extra depth of flavor.

Basting, a fancy way of saying "brushing with liquid flavorings while cooking," is another way to boost flavor. Alternatively, you can fill a spray bottle with a flavorful liquid, such as beer, wine, or juice, and spritz the food while it's cooking.

Finally, after removing the food from the grill, toss it in a sauce or glaze to finish it. All of these methods are presented in different recipes in this book. As you become more familiar with these methods of maximizing flavor, you can begin to improvise and create your own recipes to satisfy your tastes.

Building Better Marinades

By combining a few basic ingredients in a marinade, you can infuse foods with flavor. The first step is to determine the flavor profile you want to create. Herbs and spices are a good starting point. Choose dried herbs if the food will marinate for a long time, and fresh herbs if it will be cooked within twelve hours.

Next, add oil. Only a small amount of oil is needed to keep the food moist. Olive oil is frequently used, but consider more flavorful oils, such as toasted sesame oil or hot chile oil. Acidic ingredients, such as fresh citrus juice, vinegar, and wine, are essential because they work their way into the food, especially proteins, drawing out inherent flavors.

Other great additions are ingredients often referred to as aromatics: garlic, ginger, and any type of onion. A thickener, such as ketchup, prepared mustard, or tomato paste isn't always necessary, but it

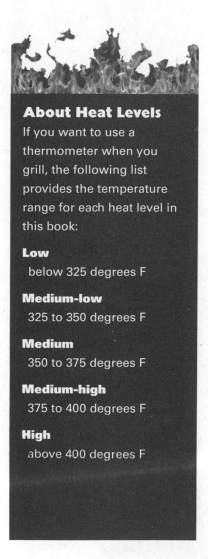

About Heat Levels

If you want to use a thermometer when you grill, the following list provides the temperature range for each heat level in this book:

Low
below 325 degrees F

Medium-low
325 to 350 degrees F

Medium
350 to 375 degrees F

Medium-high
375 to 400 degrees F

High
above 400 degrees F

can help the marinade stick to the food. It's a good idea to add a small amount of a sweetener to round out the flavors and help them work together. Liquid sweeteners, such as agave nectar, barley malt, brown rice syrup, maple syrup, or molasses, can do double duty as thickeners.

Once you've created a potent and concentrated base, add just enough broth to extend the ingredients sufficiently to soak the food. Finish the marinade with salt and ground pepper, or use alternatives that can provide even more flavor, such as tamari, vegan Worcestershire sauce, white pepper, or lemon pepper. Mix the ingredients well. Add the food and turn it until well coated. Now you have a quick and easy start on a later meal.

After placing the food in the marinade, cover the container and refrigerate until you're ready to cook. Most marinated foods can be cooked after about one hour of marinating, but for more flexibility and flavor, the food can stay in the marinade for up to three days unless a recipe indicates otherwise.

Using Wet Rubs versus Dry Rubs

Rubs, made from a combination of spices, herbs, and seasonings, can either be dry, with no liquid added, or wet, incorporating a small amount of broth, oil, wine, or other liquid. Dry rubs are a good choice for moist foods and adhere well to seitan and steamed tempeh, whereas wet rubs adhere well to dry foods and tend to work better on more permeable foods, such as portobello mushrooms or tofu.

About Wood Chips

Many different types of wood chips are available. Some of the most popular are mesquite, hickory, cherry, and apple. Each lends a different taste to foods, with the scent of the wood indicating the flavor it will add. The boldest-tasting wood is mesquite, which also burns hotter than most others, so it's a great way to generate flavor quickly. Hickory has the second strongest aroma and provides what many people think of as traditional grill flavor. Cherry and apple are milder and sweeter. A fun option is to combine various wood chips to create your own custom blend.

While shopping for wood chips, you may also see wood chunks. The chips, which are smaller and burn more quickly, are preferred for vegan cooking. Plant foods spend less time on the grill than animal-based foods; therefore, it's optimal to produce the smoke more rapidly to maximize the flavor. If you happen to have some wood chunks on hand, combine the chips and chunks in a three-to-one ratio for a longer smoke time. This type of combination is also handy for cooking several courses on the grill.

Whether dry or wet, rubs are a convenient and quick way to increase flavor because they don't require preplanning, as marinades do. A rub can be used for an initial infusion of flavor or as a finishing touch. Rubs that have a bit of sweetener tend to caramelize on the outside of the food, adding even more flavor. Just be aware that both wet and dry rubs can impart an intense flavor, so use them with care.

Using a Smoker Box

When grilling outdoors, one of the easiest ways to add flavor is by using a grill smoker box or foil packet. Smoker boxes are small metal boxes with vent holes. The box is filled with wood chips that have been soaked in water for at least thirty minutes and then is put beneath the grate, on top of the heat source. The chips catch fire, creating smoke that seeps through the holes, adding flavor to the food above. Smoke infuses the food most effectively when the grill is closed, so keep the lid shut as much as possible when using a smoker box.

Improvising a Smoker Box from Foil

For a homemade version of a smoker box, soak wood chips in water, drain them, and then wrap them in a foil packet. The packets can be kept in the freezer for impromptu grilling, and you can use them straight from the freezer. Before using the packet, poke a few holes in it with a fork.

The Art and Science of Grilling

Now that we've talked about how to boost flavor, let's take a look at some general information about grilling. For starters, be sure to familiarize yourself with your grill. All grills have hot spots. Knowing where they are will help you grill foods without charring them excessively. You can also move cooked foods to a cooler spot to more easily coordinate the timing of different components of a meal.

Before placing food on the grill, oil the grates, the food, or both. Depending on the ingredient, it's sometimes easier to oil the food, as with portobello mushrooms. To oil the grates, put a small amount of canola oil on a paper towel. Use long-handled tongs to hold the paper towel and wipe it over the grates. Be careful, as the oil may cause flare-ups and the paper towel could catch fire. Alternatively, you can mist the cold grates with cooking spray instead.

Using a thermometer is a big help in maintaining the proper temperature for cooking. Yet even if you use a thermometer, you'll probably find you need to adjust the temperature. For gas grills, if the temperature isn't hot enough, turn up the heat slightly. If it's too high, simply open the top to release some heat. For charcoal grills, if the temperature isn't high enough, partially close the top vent and allow the grill to heat up longer. (Don't close the bottom vent, as that will put the fire out.) To decrease the temperature, open the top vents or remove the cover as needed. Because it can be difficult to precisely calibrate the temperature of a grill, and because the temperature will vary over time, when following recipes always use the doneness cues, not the cooking time, as your primary reference.

The more flat the surface of the food is, the easier it is to get crisp grill marks. Clean cuts will maximize how much of the surface is in contact with the grill. To increase contact with the grill, use a turner to gently press the food against the grates. This is especially helpful with foods that aren't cut cleanly. However, be careful not to press out too much moisture. A spray bottle containing a liquid seasoning mixture is handy for replenishing moisture lost in this way.

When cooking foods that may fall between the grates, such as asparagus or green beans, you might want to use a grill sheet. Simply place the grill sheet on top of the grate and put the food on the grill sheet or follow the recipe directions. Although a grill sheet is handy, it isn't necessary. Heavy-duty grill foil will also do the trick; just be careful not tear it when turning foods. Another option is to put the food on skewers.

When making indoor variations of recipes that require grill foil, substitute regular foil. Nonstick foil is convenient, but it's almost as easy to just mist the foil with cooking spray.

Some dishes are likely to burn if placed directly on the grill grate; an example is Cinnamon Swirl (page 154), which is cooked in a skillet. To prevent burning, put an inverted cast-iron skillet on the grill to create a slightly higher cooking surface. Then put the food on top of the inverted skillet. To create an oven effect with a grill pan indoors, invert a large, heatproof bowl over the food.

Grill grates are easiest to clean while they're still warm. Be sure to use the type of brush suggested by the manufacturer of your grill. Most often, a nonabrasive brush will do the job. If you forget to clean the grill after using it, do it next time you use the grill, once it's preheated but before cooking.

Cooking outdoors may require adjustments. For example, if it's cold out, the food may take longer to cook. If using a gas grill and the propane tank is less than half full, the flame may be weaker. As you gain experience, adjusting the grill or adapting other aspects of a recipe will become second nature.

Those Deep, Dark Grill Marks

Grill marks are also sometimes called hatch marks, crosshatch marks, or hash marks. Whatever you call them, the following simple technique will help you create them like a pro in minutes. First, the grill surface has to be hot—nearly smoking hot. It also has to be well oiled so the food doesn't stick. If the food has a more presentable side (such as a portobello mushroom cap), grill that side first. Put the food on the grill, and let the grill do its work. When the food starts to slightly pull away from the grill, an indication that it's cooking, carefully lift it using a turner to assess whether the bottom is well marked. If it's not, you should be able to ease the food right back on the same ridges in the same way.

When the bottom is marked, lift the food, turn it 90 degrees (keeping the same side down), and put it back on the grill. It's important to put it on the grill just once when you turn it, as any shifting will blur the grill marks. Once the first side is crosshatched, turn the food over and cook the other side in the same way. In the interest of space, these directions aren't included in all recipes where relevant. However, this technique should be used whenever grilling portobello mushrooms, seitan, tempeh, tofu, or slabs of vegetables.

Planning Ahead

One of the best aspects of grilling is its impromptu nature. Doing a few basic tasks in advance will make it even easier to do some grilling on short notice. Tempeh and tofu benefit from some special handling, which I'll discuss shortly. Seitan, tempeh, and tofu can be marinated in the refrigerator to be grilled at your convenience. Covered, all three can be kept in their marinade in the refrigerator for up to three days. The longer they marinate, the more flavorful they'll be.

To add instant grill flavor to dishes, grill onions and roast peppers on the grill, and then keep them on hand to use in other dishes. When a recipe calls for roasted red bell peppers, it's fine to substitute store-bought roasted bell peppers; just be sure to rinse them (to remove the salty brine) and then pat them dry before using them.

To help you plan ahead, whenever a recipe calls for another recipe as an ingredient, such as a sauce or marinated protein, I've given you a heads-up just below the recipe yield to let you know what you need to prepare in advance. Likewise, the advance preparation notes will alert you whenever preparation needs to begin an hour or longer before grilling, for example, when ingredients need to marinate or dough needs to rise.

Poaching Tempeh

To mellow tempeh's somewhat bitter flavor, poach it before using it in recipes. Put about 3 inches of water in a large skillet and bring the water to a boil over high heat. Add the tempeh, decrease the temperature to low, and cook uncovered for 15 minutes. At this point the tempeh can be used as directed in a recipe. Keep in mind that hot tempeh absorbs flavors more readily than cold tempeh does, so if you're marinating the tempeh, cut it and put it in the marinade as soon as it's cool enough to handle.

Pressing Tofu

I almost always have tofu marinating in the refrigerator. Most of the recipes in this book call for extra-firm tofu. For tofu to absorb flavors, its moisture should be pressed out before it's marinated. Cut the tofu as directed in the recipe or into four slabs. Put the tofu between paper towels (or wrap it in a clean dish towel) on a plate or cutting board. Put a second plate or cutting board on top of the tofu. Put the tofu in the refrigerator and let it sit for at least 1 hour or longer before using it as directed in a recipe. The water content in tofu can vary depending on brand and variety, and it may be necessary to change the towels if they become soaked.

Grilling Onions

To grill onions, preheat a grill, grill pan, or electric grill to medium heat. Cut the onions into 1/2-inch-thick rounds, lightly mist them with olive oil spray, and sprinkle with salt and pepper. Put the onions on the grill and cook until marked, about 4 minutes. Turn over and cook until the other side is marked, about 4 minutes. (If using an electric grill, keep it open and cook a few minutes longer if necessary.) Stored in a covered container in the refrigerator, grilled onions will keep for 1 week.

Roasting Bell Peppers and Chiles

To roast bell peppers or chiles outdoors, preheat a grill to high heat. Cut the peppers in half lengthwise. Remove the stems and seeds unless directed otherwise in the recipe. Lightly brush the peppers with olive oil, then put them on the grill cut-side down. Close the lid and cook until blackened, about 10 minutes, turning as necessary to blacken all sides. To prepare them indoors, preheat the broiler. Line a 13 x 9-inch baking pan with foil for easier cleanup. Prepare the peppers as for an outdoor grill, then place them in the pan cut-side down. Broil for about 8 minutes, turning as necessary, until evenly blackened. It's preferable to overblacken rather than underblacken, as this will make it easier to remove the skins. Chiles are often used at this point (with blackened skins) unless a recipe requires that the skins be removed.

To remove the skins, transfer the peppers to a bowl while they're still hot. Cover tightly with plastic wrap and let sit for about 20 minutes to allow the peppers to steam. This will loosen the skins. Using your fingers and a paring knife, remove and discard the skins. Stored in a covered container in the refrigerator, roasted peppers will keep for 1 week.

A Quick Peek in the Pantry

You'll find information about some specific ingredients, especially those that are unusual, in the Glossary (page 179). However, I thought you might find it helpful to know a little about some of the more common ingredients that I always keep in my kitchen.

Beans. Canned beans are wonderfully convenient, and I always have some in the pantry. If you have the time, it's even better to cook a big pot of beans and store them in the freezer in $1\frac{1}{2}$-cup portions (about the amount in a typical can of beans). Stored in a covered container in the freezer, cooked beans will keep for 3 months.

Broth. If you make your own vegetable broth, good for you! If not, there are several vegan boxed broths on the market. They vary in how salty they are, so don't add salt until you've added the broth, and then judiciously season with salt to taste. I prefer using salt-free vegetable broth.

Fruits and vegetables. When they are affordable, I buy organic fruit and vegetables. Look for locally grown vegetables in season too. Farmers' markets are great places for finding the very freshest and best-tasting produce.

Herbs and spices. Dried herbs and spices are best used within a year of purchase. If possible, purchase them loose rather than packaged. This allows you to buy smaller amounts for enhanced freshness, and it's usually more economical too.

Oils. Like many health-conscious cooks, I make an effort to use as little oil as possible. However, marinades do need some oil to help the food absorb flavors. The most frequently used oils in this book are olive oil, canola oil, and toasted sesame oil. Unless otherwise stated, regular olive oil is fine. I only use the more pricey extra-virgin olive oil when it won't be heated, to showcase its delicate flavor and protect its monounsaturated fats. When oiling a grill, grill pan, or electric grill, canola oil and cooking spray may be used interchangeably. When oil is being directly applied to food, olive oil is a better choice. You can brush it on, use store-bought olive oil spray, or use a refillable oil spray bottle.

Vinegars. With their acidic profiles, vinegars brighten the flavors of marinades and sauces beautifully. Balsamic vinegar, cider vinegar, distilled white vinegar, red wine vinegar, seasoned rice vinegar, white wine vinegar, and others all bring different intensities and levels of sharpness to recipes. In creating your own marinade recipes or adapting these recipes, start with a small amount of vinegar and add more to taste. Excessive amounts of vinegar can overwhelm the taste buds.

Wines. Some of these recipes call for wine, which can lend added complexity to the flavor of a dish. Wine is also touted for having umami: that combination of sour, salty, bitter, and sweet that surpasses each of these individual components for the ultimate savory taste experience. However, if you'd prefer not to use wine, substitute an equal amount of broth. For red wines, add 1 teaspoon of red wine vinegar for each ½ cup of wine called for in a recipe. For white wines, add 1 teaspoon of lemon juice or white wine vinegar for each ½ cup of wine called for.

In Case You Missed It

People generally don't read cookbooks from cover to cover, so let me reiterate a few important points to help you get the most from your grill:
- Know your grill. They all have hot and cool spots.
- For optimal results, cook according to the doneness cues rather than the suggested times.
- Be sure to read Those Deep, Dark Grill Marks (page 13) for pointers on how to ensure perfect crosshatching.

- Use foil smoke packets (see page 11) to increase flavor.
- When using an electric grill, use the ridged grill plates unless otherwise specified in the recipe.
- Most importantly, have fun and experiment! These recipes are just a starting point.

Grilling for Any Occasion

With the following suggested menus, you can make any occasion an opportunity for grilling. Of course, you can also simply mix and match recipes that seem appealing, but to help you get started, here are a few of my favorite combinations.

Grazing Menu

Lettuce Wraps (page 44)
Polenta Stacks (page 40)
Grilled Jicama Rounds with Black Beans (page 28)
Tomato-Arugula Flatbread (page 35)

Mother's Day Brunch

Maple-Glazed Grapefruit (page 140)
Fresh Herb Frittata (page 102)
Oh-So-Easy Hash Browns (page 136)

Father's Day Dinner

Seitan-Potato Sticks (page 99)
Garlicky Cauliflower (page 131)
Rocky Road Flatbread (page 152)

Summer Cookout

Black Bean Burgers (page 66) with Spiced Ketchup (page 164)
Lemony Greek Barley Salad (page 128)
Skillet-Grilled Cherry Crisp (page 148)

Fourth of July Feast

Skillet-Grilled Breadsticks (page 38)
Coffee-Crusted Ribz (page 96)
Roasted Corn on the Cob with Flavored Butters (page 130)
Grilled Radicchio Salad (page 124)
Spicy Red Potato and Bell Pepper Salad (page 127)
Fruit Salsa with Sweet Cinnamon Chips (page 142)

Midsummer's Night Dinner

Sparkling Margaritas (page 45)

Roasted Corn Chowder (page 50)

Panzanella with Tempeh (page 77)

Skillet-Grilled Mango-Blueberry Cobbler (page 147)

Impress the Neighbors

Charred Leek Spread with Dill on Baguette Rounds (page 29)

Romaine and Asparagus Salad (page 125)

Savory Grilled Tofu with Mushroom Sauce (page 86)

Pineapple and Pomegranate Couscous Cakes (page 150)

Mexican Fiesta

Stuffed Jalapeño Chiles (page 27)

Red Bell Pepper Gazpacho (page 48)

Mexican Seitan Sandwiches (page 59)

Mexican S'mores (page 151)

A Day in the French Countryside

Olives with Herbs (page 21)

Grilled Ratatouille (page 132)

Rosemary Flatbread (page 36)

An Asian-Inspired Evening

Asian Asparagus and Chinese Cabbage (page 24)

Five-Spice Tofu (page 83)

Asian Sesame Noodles (page 138)

Grilled Nectarines with Five-Spice Granola (page 146)

Chapter 2
Scrumptious Starters and Small Plates

Roasting garlic brings out its subtle sweetness. Serve the mashed garlic with bread, or add a bit to grain dishes, pasta dishes, sauces, or soups to quickly imbue them with rich, enticing flavor.

ROASTED GARLIC

Yield: 2 heads, 4 servings

2 large heads garlic
(see Cook Smart)

2 sprigs fresh thyme, rosemary,
oregano, or a combination
(optional)

1 tablespoon olive oil

¼ teaspoon salt

Pinch ground pepper

Outdoor Method

Preheat an outdoor grill to medium-high heat.

Cut the tops off the garlic heads and peel some of the skins back to expose the cloves. Tear off one 12-inch piece of foil. Put the optional thyme on the foil. Put the garlic on the thyme and drizzle with the oil. Then sprinkle with the salt and pepper. Wrap the foil around the garlic and put the packet on the grill. Cook until the garlic is soft and lightly browned, about 25 minutes.

Discard the thyme. To serve, gently pry the cloves from the skin with a fork. Transfer the cloves to a cutting board and mash with the side of a knife. Transfer to a bowl for serving. Stored in a covered container in the refrigerator, the garlic (mashed or as whole cloves) will keep for 2 weeks.

Indoor Method

Preheat the oven to 400 degrees F. Wrap the garlic and other ingredients as directed. Bake until the garlic is soft and lightly browned, about 25 minutes

Per serving: 50 calories, 2 g protein, 3 g fat (1 g sat), 5 g carbs, 143 mg sodium, 10 mg calcium, 2 g fiber

Cook Smart

- Elephant garlic, which has large cloves, is a good choice for roasting. So is extra-hardy German garlic, if available.

One of the simplest recipes in this book, these olives are easily customized to fit any menu. Many grocery stores offer various olives in bulk, allowing you to conveniently purchase an assortment. Select a variety of different olives for this recipe for the most colorful and festive presentation.

OLIVES WITH HERBS

Yield: 4 servings

¾ cup pitted olives, any variety

2 sprigs fresh thyme

1 sprig fresh rosemary

1 clove garlic, minced

Pinch red pepper flakes

1 tablespoon dry red wine or salt-free vegetable broth

Outdoor Method

Preheat an outdoor grill to medium-high heat.

Tear off one 18-inch piece of foil. Arrange the olives in a single layer on the foil. Top with the thyme, rosemary, garlic, and red pepper flakes. Fold up the sides of the foil to form a rim, then pour the wine over the olives. Fold the packet closed and put it on the grill. Cook for 10 minutes, turning the packet over halfway through the cooking time.

Indoor Method

Preheat the oven to 400 degrees F. Prepare and wrap the olives and other ingredients as directed. Bake for 10 minutes, turning the packet over halfway through the baking time.

Per serving: 24 calories, 0 g protein, 2 g fat (0.3 g sat), 2 g carbs, 105 mg sodium, 22 mg calcium, 1 g fiber

OLIVES WITH MEXICAN HERBS: Substitute a sprig of fresh oregano for the rosemary. Add 1 tablespoon minced jalapeño chile and an additional clove of garlic.

These luscious bites have a Mediterranean taste, thanks to the vibrant dressing. Nutritional yeast contributes a richness that balances well with the flavor from the grill.

GRILLED BABY ARTICHOKES

See photo facing page 44.

Yield: 6 servings

Mediterranean Dressing

1 shallot, minced

Juice from ½ lemon

1 tablespoon minced capers

1 tablespoon balsamic vinegar

1 teaspoon nutritional yeast
   flakes

Artichokes

2 tablespoons distilled white
   vinegar

15 baby artichokes (see Cook
   Smart)

1 tablespoon olive oil

¼ teaspoon salt

Pinch ground pepper

To make the dressing, put all the ingredients in a small bowl and whisk to combine.

To prepare the artichokes, fill a medium bowl two-thirds full with cold water. Stir in the vinegar.

Working with the artichokes one at a time, remove the outer leaves until you reach the inner yellowish leaves. Trim ½ inch off the top and cut off almost the entire stem, leaving just enough stem so the choke stays intact. Cut the artichoke in half lengthwise and scoop out the hairy core. Put each artichoke in the vinegar water immediately after preparing it to prevent browning.

Fill a medium saucepan two-thirds full with salted water and bring to a boil over high heat. Drain the artichokes and put them in the saucepan. Decrease the heat to medium-low and simmer uncovered until nearly tender, about 7 minutes. Drain well and transfer to a medium bowl. Drizzle with the oil and sprinkle with the salt and pepper. Toss gently until the artichokes are evenly coated.

Preheat a grill, grill pan, or electric grill to medium-high heat.

Working in batches if necessary, put the artichokes on the grill cut-side down and cook until marked, about 6 minutes. (If using an electric grill, keep it open and cook a few minutes longer if necessary.)

Transfer the artichokes to a bowl as they are cooked. While the artichokes are hot, pour the dressing over them, whisking it first if it has separated, and toss gently to coat. Serve hot or at room temperature.

Per serving: 94 calories, 6 g protein, 2 g fat (0.3 g sat), 17 g carbs, 314 mg sodium, 6 mg calcium, 8 g fiber

Cook Smart

- It's possible to use canned artichoke hearts in this recipe, which decreases prep time. If you choose to do so, be sure to rinse and drain them well and then pat them with a clean kitchen towel until very dry.
- To make this elegant dish in advance, prepare everything up to the grilling step. Stored in separate covered containers in the refrigerator, the dressing and simmered artichokes will each keep for 2 days.
- If you have leftovers, chop the grilled artichokes and add them to pasta dishes, salads, sandwiches, or pizzas.

In many parts of the country, asparagus comes into season just as intrepid home chefs become eager to brave early grilling. Light and flavorful, this pleasantly crunchy, fresh dish is a wonderful way to welcome spring.

ASIAN ASPARAGUS AND CHINESE CABBAGE

Yield: 4 servings

8 ounces asparagus, trimmed

1 teaspoon canola oil

¼ teaspoon salt

⅛ teaspoon ground pepper

1 cup thinly sliced Chinese cabbage

1 teaspoon toasted sesame seeds

1 teaspoon reduced-sodium tamari

1 teaspoon seasoned rice vinegar

½ teaspoon toasted sesame oil

Preheat a grill, grill pan, or electric grill to medium heat.

Put the asparagus in a medium bowl. Drizzle with the canola oil and sprinkle with the salt and pepper. Toss gently until the asparagus is evenly coated. Put the asparagus on the grill and cook, turning occasionally, until marked, tender, and bright green, about 8 minutes. (If using an electric grill, keep it open and cook a few minutes longer if necessary.)

When the asparagus spears are cool enough to handle, cut them into 1-inch pieces. Put the asparagus, cabbage, sesame seeds, tamari, vinegar, and sesame oil in a medium bowl and toss gently to coat.

Cover and refrigerate for at least 30 minutes to allow the flavors to meld.

Per serving: 42 calories, 2 g protein, 3 g fat (0.2 g sat), 3 g carbs, 92 mg sodium, 78 mg calcium, 2 g fiber

ASIAN ASPARAGUS SPEARS: For a warm asparagus side dish, leave the asparagus in stalks. Omit the cabbage and toss the asparagus spears with the sesame seeds, tamari, vinegar, and sesame oil as soon as they come off the grill.

I rarely use button mushrooms, opting for more flavorful varieties, but they are a terrific canvas for the bold seasonings here. However, you can use cremini mushrooms if you prefer. Either way, the mushrooms will be moist and bursting with the flavors of the bayou.

CAJUN MUSHROOMS

Yield: 4 servings

1 tablespoon olive oil

8 ounces button mushrooms, cut into halves or quarters if large

1 tablespoon minced shallot

2 cloves garlic, minced

½ teaspoon smoked paprika

½ teaspoon dried thyme

¼ teaspoon ground cumin

¼ teaspoon salt

Pinch ground pepper

2 tablespoons cider vinegar

1 tablespoon hot sauce

Outdoor Method

Preheat an outdoor grill to medium-low heat and put a large cast-iron skillet on the grill.

Put the oil in the skillet. Add the mushrooms and shallot and stir to coat. Close the grill and cook, stirring occasionally, until the mushrooms start to change color, about 7 minutes. Add the garlic, paprika, thyme, cumin, salt, and pepper and cook, stirring constantly, for 1 to 2 minutes to lightly toast the spices. Add the vinegar and hot sauce and stir to coat the mushrooms. Cook for 1 minute, stirring occasionally. Serve hot or at room temperature.

Indoor Method

Cook the mushrooms in a large skillet on the stove following the same instructions.

Per serving: 50 calories, 2 g protein, 4 g fat (0.5 g sat), 3 g carbs, 172 mg sodium, 6 mg calcium, 1 g fiber

Cook Smart

• If you happen to have leftovers, the mushrooms are a great burger topping.

In this recipe, bite-sized potatoes are dressed with vegan sour cream seasoned with herbs, which provides a tasty counterpoint to the grill flavors. This crowd-pleaser is popular with people of all ages.

RED POTATOES WITH DILL CREAM

Yield: 4 servings

1½ pounds small red potatoes, scrubbed

1 tablespoon olive oil

½ teaspoon salt, plus more as desired

¼ teaspoon ground pepper, plus more as desired

¾ cup vegan sour cream

2 teaspoons minced fresh dill, or ½ teaspoon dried dill weed

1 teaspoon minced fresh chives, or ¼ teaspoon dried

1 clove garlic, minced

Put the potatoes in a large saucepan and add cold water to cover. Bring to a boil over medium-high heat. Decrease the heat to medium and cook uncovered until fork-tender, about 16 minutes. Drain and let cool.

When the potatoes are cool enough to handle, cut them in half using a serrated knife and put them in a large bowl. Drizzle with the oil and sprinkle with the salt and pepper. Stir gently until the potatoes are evenly coated. You can proceed with the recipe at this point, or you can store the potatoes in a covered container in the refrigerator for up to 24 hours.

Put the vegan sour cream, dill, chives, and garlic in a small bowl and stir to combine. Season with salt and pepper to taste. The mixture can be used immediately or may be stored in a covered container in the refrigerator for up to 4 days.

Preheat a grill, grill pan, or electric grill to medium-high heat.

Put the potatoes on the grill cut-side down and cook until marked, about 5 minutes. (If using an electric grill, keep it open and cook a few minutes longer if necessary.)

Serve immediately, drizzled with the vegan sour cream mixture.

Per serving: 282 calories, 5 g protein, 11 g fat (4 g sat), 41 g carbs, 535 mg sodium, 16 mg calcium, 3 g fiber

These are over-the-top spicy, so be prepared. Any leftover filling can be eaten as a flavorful cracker spread. For less adventurous palates, try stuffing poblano chiles instead, as they are much milder than jalapeños. (They are also much larger, so fewer will be needed.)

STUFFED JALAPEÑO CHILES

Yield: 8 chiles, 4 servings

4 ounces smoked tofu, homemade (page 87 or 88) or store-bought, crumbled

2 tablespoons vegan mayonnaise

1 tablespoon nutritional yeast flakes

1 tablespoon unsweetened soy milk

1 teaspoon ume plum vinegar

1 tablespoon minced red onion

2 teaspoons toasted sunflower seeds

8 jalapeño chiles

½ cup salsa, for serving

Soak eight wooden toothpicks in water for 30 minutes. Preheat a grill, grill pan, or electric grill to medium-high heat.

Put the tofu, vegan mayonnaise, nutritional yeast, soy milk, and vinegar in a small blender or food processor and process until smooth. Transfer to a small bowl and stir in the onion and sunflower seeds.

Carefully cut one side off each chile, forming a canoe shape. Reserve the cut-off pieces. Remove the seeds from the chiles and stuff each with about 1 tablespoon of the filling. Put the cut pieces back on the chiles and skewer with the toothpicks to hold them together. Lightly mist the chiles with olive oil spray.

Put the chiles on the grill and cook, turning occasionally, until soft and slightly charred, about 14 minutes. (If using an electric grill, keep it open and cook a few minutes longer if necessary.)

For each serving, put 2 tablespoons of the salsa on a plate and top with 2 chiles. Serve at once.

Per serving: 170 calories, 10 g protein, 10 g fat (2 g sat), 8 g carbs, 584 mg sodium, 84 mg calcium, 2 g fiber

These nifty rounds, infused with classic Southwestern flavors, are a nutritious appetizer that can be served hot or at room temperature.

GRILLED JICAMA ROUNDS WITH BLACK BEANS

Yield: 6 servings ● *Advance prep: Marinate the jicama for 1 hour.*

Marinated Jicama

1 tablespoon reduced-
   sodium tamari
1 tablespoon seasoned
   rice vinegar
1 teaspoon olive oil
¼ teaspoon liquid smoke
1 jicama, peeled and cut
   into ⅛-inch-thick rounds

Black Bean Topping

1 (15-ounce) can black beans,
   drained and rinsed
1 carrot, shredded
½ poblano chile, seeded
   and minced
3 tablespoons minced
   red onion
1 tablespoon seasoned
   rice vinegar
2 cloves garlic, minced
1 teaspoon extra-virgin
   olive oil
1 teaspoon reduced-
   sodium tamari
½ teaspoon dried oregano
Salt
Ground pepper
1 avocado, diced, for garnish

To prepare the jicama, put the tamari, vinegar, oil, and liquid smoke in a 13 x 9-inch nonreactive baking pan and stir to combine. Add the jicama and turn to coat. Let marinate at room temperature for 1 hour, turning the jicama occasionally.

To prepare the topping, put the beans, carrot, chile, onion, vinegar, garlic, oil, tamari, and oregano in a medium bowl. Stir gently, taking care not to crush the beans. Season with salt and pepper to taste.

To grill the jicama and assemble the rounds, preheat a grill, grill pan, or electric grill to medium-high heat.

Lightly oil the grill with canola oil. Put the jicama on the grill, reserving the marinade. Cook until marked, about 4 minutes, while occasionally basting with the marinade. Turn over and cook in the same fashion until the other side is marked, about 3 minutes longer. (If using an electric grill, keep it open and cook a few minutes longer if necessary.)

Put the jicama on serving plates and top each round with a heaping ¼ cup of the bean mixture and a few pieces of the avocado.

Per serving: 184 calories, 7 g protein, 6 g fat (1 g sat), 29 g carbs, 467 mg sodium, 42 mg calcium, 11 g fiber

Note: Analysis doesn't include salt and ground pepper to taste.

Cook Smart

• For a fancy garnish, top each round with 2 tablespoons of Avocado Sauce (page 173) instead of the chopped avocado.

Leeks are a member of the onion and garlic family, perhaps best known for their use in potato-leek soup. Because of how they are grown, dirt tends to become lodged between the layers, so they must be washed well (see Cook Smart). If you can track down vegan blue cheese crumbles, sprinkle them over the spread before topping with the apple slices to take this appetizer over the top.

CHARRED LEEK SPREAD
WITH DILL ON BAGUETTE ROUNDS

Yield: 4 servings • Advance prep: Soak the cashews for 1 hour.

Leek Spread

¼ cup raw cashews, soaked in cold water for 1 hour and drained

2 tablespoons water

1 tablespoon freshly squeezed lemon juice

1 tablespoon cider vinegar

2 teaspoons nutritional yeast flakes

½ cup vegan mayonnaise

2 tablespoons minced red bell pepper

2 teaspoons minced fresh dill, or ½ teaspoon dried dill weed

1 clove garlic, minced

¼ teaspoon salt

Pinch ground pepper

1 leek, white part only (about 4 inches), washed well (see Cook Smart)

Accompaniments

1 baguette, cut into 1-inch-thick slices

1 Granny Smith apple, cored and thinly sliced

To make the spread, put the cashews, water, lemon juice, vinegar, and nutritional yeast in a small blender and process until completely smooth. Transfer to a small bowl and stir in the vegan mayonnaise, bell pepper, dill, garlic, salt, and pepper.

Preheat a grill, grill pan, or electric grill to medium-high heat.

Lightly oil the grill with canola oil. Put the leek on the grill and cook until marked, about 5 minutes. Turn over and cook until the other side is marked, about 5 minutes. (If using an electric grill, keep it open and cook a few minutes longer if necessary.)

When the leek is cool enough to handle, slice it thinly. Add it to the cashew mixture and stir to combine. The spread can be used immediately or may be stored in a covered container in the refrigerator for up to 3 days.

To assemble the rounds, spread a scant tablespoon of the leek mixture on each slice of baguette. Top each with a slice of the apple. Serve immediately.

Per serving: 250 calories, 4 g protein, 12 g fat (1 g sat), 17 g carbs, 399 mg sodium, 11 mg calcium, 2 g fiber

Cook Smart

• To clean leeks, cut off the dark green leaves. Slice halfway into the leek lengthwise so you can gently open it like a book. Fill a bowl with cold water. Put the leek in the bowl and, while gently holding the layers apart, swish it through the water. Rinse well to remove any dirt still clinging to the leaves. Cut off the root end and prepare the white part as directed in the recipe.

If you like guacamole, you'll love grilled guacamole. In this recipe, grilled avocados are mixed with sweet red onion and smoky chipotle chile in adobo sauce to create a dip with deep, satisfying flavors. Because prepared avocados tend to discolor, this is best eaten within a few hours of making it.

GRILLED GUACAMOLE

Yield: 1 cup, 4 servings

6 teaspoons freshly
    squeezed lemon juice

½ teaspoon olive oil

2 avocados, halved, left in
    the skin, and pitted

½ cup minced grilled red
    onion (see page 14)

2 cloves garlic, minced

1 teaspoon minced chipotle
    chile in adobo sauce

Salt (optional)

Ground pepper (optional)

Tortilla chips, for serving

Preheat a grill, grill pan, or electric grill to medium-high heat.

Put 1½ teaspoons of the lemon juice and the oil in a small bowl and mix well. Brush the mixture on the cut side of the avocados. Put the avocados on the grill cut-side down and cook until marked, about 3 minutes. (If using an electric grill, keep it open and cook a few minutes longer if necessary.)

Scoop the avocado flesh into a medium bowl with a large spoon and mash well with a fork or potato masher. Stir in the onion, garlic, chile, and remaining lemon juice. Season with salt and pepper to taste. Serve with tortilla chips for dipping.

Per serving: 128 calories, 2 g protein, 12 g fat (2 g sat), 7 g carbs, 16 mg sodium, 10 mg calcium, 5 g fiber

Note: Analysis doesn't include salt and ground pepper to taste or tortilla chips for serving.

TWO-PEPPER GRILLED GUACAMOLE: If you love spicy food, grill a jalapeño chile while grilling the avocados. Cut off the stem, mince the chile, and stir it in with the onion.

Slightly reminiscent of the filling in deviled eggs but far better tasting and more healthful, this spread is featured in The Veg Wedge (page 56). It's also perfect to offer when guests arrive or when hungry kids get home from school. For a quick fix, serve it with whole-grain crackers rather than grilled bread.

DEVILED SPREAD WITH GRILLED CROSTINI

Yield: 1 cup spread, 8 servings • *Advance prep: Press the tofu.*

Deviled Spread

8 ounces extra-firm tofu, pressed (see page 14) and crumbled

2 tablespoons vegan mayonnaise

1 tablespoon nutritional yeast flakes

1 tablespoon minced pepperoncini

1½ teaspoons prepared spicy mustard (see Cook Smart)

1 teaspoon red wine vinegar

¼ teaspoon salt

¼ teaspoon ground pepper

Crostini

1 baguette, cut into 1-inch-thick slices

2 tablespoons olive oil

To make the spread, put all the ingredients in a small bowl and mash with a fork until evenly combined. The spread can be used immediately or may be stored in a covered container in the refrigerator for up to 1 week.

To prepare the crostini, preheat a grill, grill pan, or electric grill to medium heat.

Brush one side of the baguette slices with the oil. Working in batches if necessary, put the baguette slices on the grill oil-side down and cook until marked, about 4 minutes. Turn over and cook until the other side is marked, about 3 minutes. (If using an electric grill, keep it open and cook a few minutes longer if necessary.)

To serve, put the spread in a bowl in the center of a platter and arrange the crostini around it oiled-side up.

Per serving: 224 calories, 7 g protein, 8 g fat (2 g sat), 12 g carbs, 375 mg sodium, 38 mg calcium, 1 g fiber

Cook Smart

• Spicy mustard, sometimes called Cajun mustard, can be found in the condiment aisle in most supermarkets. If it's something you won't use often, you can substitute prepared yellow mustard and add ⅛ to ¼ teaspoon ground cayenne to the spread.

POBLANO BRUSCHETTA

Yield: 4 servings

3 roasted poblano chiles
(see page 14), chopped

2 tablespoons minced
red onion

Juice from ½ lime

2 cloves garlic, minced

2 teaspoons minced
fresh cilantro

1 teaspoon minced
fresh oregano, or
¼ teaspoon dried

1 teaspoon balsamic vinegar

¼ teaspoon salt

⅛ teaspoon ground pepper

Pinch red pepper flakes

½ baguette

2 teaspoons olive oil

½ teaspoon ancho chile
powder

1 large tomato, preferably
heirloom, cut into
½-inch-thick slices

Put the chiles, onion, lime juice, garlic, cilantro, oregano, vinegar, salt, pepper, and red pepper flakes in a medium bowl and stir to combine.

Preheat a grill, grill pan, or electric grill to medium heat.

Cut the baguette in half lengthwise. Put the oil and chile powder in a small bowl and stir to combine. Brush the oil over the cut sides of the baguette. Put the baguette on the grill, oiled-side down, and cook until marked, about 3 minutes. (If using an electric grill, keep it open and cook a few minutes longer if necessary.)

To serve, distribute the tomato slices equally over each baguette half; if the slices are wider than the baguette, cut them in half. Spread the poblano mixture evenly over the tomato and cut each baguette half into four equal pieces.

Per serving: 197 calories, 4 g protein, 5 g fat (0.3 g sat), 22 g carbs, 388 mg sodium, 23 mg calcium, 4 g fiber

Tender, juicy portobello mushrooms get star treatment in this gourmet recipe. Mushroom lovers will adore the hearty grill flavor accented with thyme.

PORTOBELLO BRUSCHETTA

Yield: 6 servings

12 ounces portobello mushrooms, stemmed and cut into ½-inch-thick slices (see Cook Smart)

2 red bell peppers, cut into ½-inch-thick rings

2 shallots, cut into ½-inch-thick slices

2 teaspoons minced capers

2 teaspoons balsamic vinegar

1 teaspoon minced fresh thyme, or ¼ teaspoon dried

¼ teaspoon salt

Pinch ground cayenne

Pinch ground pepper

12 slices French bread, about 1 inch thick

2 teaspoons extra-virgin olive oil

Cook Smart

• If you want to save time and ease preparation, look for sliced portobello mushrooms at your market.

Outdoor Method

Cover a small section of an outdoor grill with foil and lightly mist it with cooking spray. Preheat the grill to medium-high heat.

Lightly oil the uncovered section of the grill with canola oil. Put the mushrooms on the grill and cook until marked, about 5 minutes. Turn over and cook until the other side is marked, about 5 minutes. Transfer the mushrooms to a medium bowl. Put the bell peppers on the grill. Put the shallots on the foil. Close the grill and cook until the bell peppers are marked on the bottom, 4 to 5 minutes.

Chop the bell peppers and mince the shallots. Put the mushrooms, bell peppers, shallots, capers, vinegar, thyme, salt, cayenne, and pepper in a medium bowl and stir gently to combine.

Put the bread on the grill and cook until marked on the bottom, 2 to 3 minutes. Transfer to a serving platter and top evenly with the mushroom mixture. Drizzle with the oil and serve.

Indoor Method

Preheat a grill pan or electric grill to medium-high heat.

Lightly oil the grill with canola oil. Put the mushrooms on the grill pan or grill and cook until marked, about 8 minutes. Turn over and cook until the other side is marked, about 6 minutes. (If using an electric grill, keep it open for all the vegetables and cook a few minutes longer if necessary.) Put the bell peppers and shallots on the grill pan or grill and cook until marked on the bottom, about 7 minutes. Proceed with the recipe as directed.

Per serving: 291 calories, 10 g protein, 2 g fat (0.2 g sat), 55 g carbs, 640 mg sodium, 49 mg calcium, 4 g fiber

Here's the best of summer on a piece of bread. In this recipe, smoky tomatoes are topped with dollops of fresh-tasting pesto for a delightful contrast in flavor and color. In addition to being a mouthwatering appetizer, these tomatoes are an essential ingredient in Pesto Pasta with Tomatoes (page 108).

PESTO-TOPPED TOMATOES

Yield: 4 servings • *Advance prep: Make Pine Nut Pesto (page 108).*

8 Roma tomatoes, cut in half and seeded

1 tablespoon olive oil

2 cloves garlic, minced

1 teaspoon Italian seasoning blend

½ teaspoon smoked salt

⅛ teaspoon ground pepper

4 teaspoons Pine Nut Pesto (page 108)

1 baguette, cut into 1-inch-thick slices

Preheat a grill, grill pan, or electric grill to medium-high heat.

Put the tomatoes, oil, garlic, Italian seasoning blend, salt, and pepper in a large bowl. Stir gently until the tomatoes are evenly coated.

Put the tomatoes on the grill skin-side down. Cook until marked, about 4 minutes. Turn over and cook until the other side is marked, about 3 minutes. (If using an electric grill, keep it open and cook a few minutes longer if necessary.)

Transfer the tomatoes to a serving platter, placing them cut-side up. Top each with ¼ teaspoon of the pesto. Serve with the baguette slices on the side.

Per serving: 359 calories, 11 g protein, 8 g fat (1 g sat), 38 g carbs, 498 mg sodium, 12 mg calcium, 5 g fiber

Rosemary-and-chive-seasoned tomatoes sit atop peppery arugula, taking this flatbread to the next level. The pungent horseradish sauce provides the ideal piquant finish.

TOMATO-ARUGULA FLATBREAD

Yield: One 12-inch flatbread, 4 servings
Advance prep: Make Rosemary Flatbread (page 36) and Creamy Horseradish Sauce (page 172).

12 ounces tomatoes, preferably heirloom, seeded and chopped

1 tablespoon minced fresh chives

2 teaspoons balsamic vinegar

1 teaspoon extra-virgin olive oil

1 teaspoon minced fresh rosemary

1 clove garlic, minced

½ teaspoon Italian seasoning blend

¼ teaspoon salt

Pinch ground pepper

2 cups arugula, lightly packed and chopped

1 Rosemary Flatbread (page 36), grilled or baked

3 tablespoons Creamy Horseradish Sauce (page 172)

Outdoor Method

Preheat an outdoor grill to medium-high heat.

Put the tomatoes, chives, vinegar, oil, rosemary, garlic, Italian seasoning blend, salt, and pepper in a medium bowl and stir gently to combine.

Spread the arugula evenly over the flatbread. Put the flatbread on the grill and cook just until the arugula wilts, 3 to 4 minutes. Remove from the grill and top evenly with the tomato mixture. Drizzle the horseradish sauce evenly over the top. Cut into wedges and serve at once.

Indoor Method

Preheat the oven to 425 degrees F. After topping the flatbread with the arugula, bake for about 4 minutes, just until the arugula wilts. Proceed with the recipe as directed.

Per serving: 247 calories, 5 g protein, 9 g fat (1 g sat), 35 g carbs, 556 mg sodium, 173 mg calcium, 3 g fiber

Sometimes known as the remembrance herb, rosemary is a member of the mint family native to the Mediterranean region. A tidbit of folklore is that tucking a sprig of rosemary under your pillow can prevent nightmares. I'm not sure how well that works, but I do guarantee that rosemary makes for outstanding flavor in this flatbread.

ROSEMARY FLATBREAD

Yield: One 12-inch flatbread, 4 servings ● Advance prep: The dough must rise for 1½ hours.

1¼ cups all-purpose flour, plus more if needed

4 teaspoons minced fresh rosemary, or 1 teaspoon dried

½ teaspoon salt

¼ teaspoon ground pepper

½ cup warm water (about 105 degrees F), plus more if needed

1 teaspoon active dry yeast

½ teaspoon agave nectar

1 tablespoon olive oil

Put the flour, rosemary, salt, and pepper in a medium bowl and stir to combine.

Put the water, yeast, and agave nectar in a small bowl and stir to combine. Set aside for 5 minutes to proof; the yeast is ready when the mixture bubbles. Stir in the oil. Pour into the flour mixture and stir well to form a cohesive dough. If necessary, add more water or flour, 1 tablespoon at a time, until the dough comes together and is firm enough to knead.

Turn the dough out onto a lightly floured work surface and knead until smooth, about 7 minutes. Form the dough into a ball.

Lightly mist a medium bowl with cooking spray. Put the dough in the bowl and turn to coat with the oil. Cover with a clean kitchen towel and let rise in a warm place until doubled in size, about 1½ hours (see Cook Smart, page 39).

Outdoor Method

Preheat an outdoor grill to medium-high heat.

Lightly flour a 16-inch piece of parchment paper. Put the dough on the parchment paper and roll it out to a 12-inch round. Lightly oil the grill with canola oil. Carefully transfer the dough to the grill by inverting it onto the grill and then peeling off the parchment paper. Keep the lid open and cook until marked, about 3 minutes. Turn over and cook until the other side is marked, about 3 minutes.

Indoor Method

Preheat a grill pan to medium-high heat. Grill as directed, cooking the bread until marked on both sides, 4 to 5 minutes per side.

Alternatively, the flatbread can be baked in the oven. Preheat the oven to 400 degrees F. After rolling out the dough, transfer it to a baking sheet, keeping it on the parchment paper for easier cleanup. Prick the dough several times with a fork to prevent it from puffing up. Bake for about 7 minutes, until golden brown.

Per serving: 158 calories, 4 g protein, 3 g fat (1 g sat), 28 g carbs, 285 mg sodium, 3 mg calcium, 1 g fiber

MIDDLE EASTERN FLATBREAD: Add 1 teaspoon zaatar (a Middle Eastern herb-and-spice mixture) to the flour mixture.

THYME FLATBREAD: Substitute minced fresh thyme for the rosemary.

In this era of convenience, store-bought bread has, sadly, become the norm. Of course, the spongy white loaves that pass as bread can never replace authentic, home-baked versions. The aroma and flavor of freshly baked bread is so comforting, and when savory notes from grilling are added to the experience, the results are almost magical.

SKILLET-GRILLED BREADSTICKS

Yield: 10 breadsticks, 5 servings ● *Advance prep: The dough must rise for 2 hours.*

1½ cups all-purpose flour, plus more if needed

1 tablespoon vital wheat gluten

1 teaspoon Italian seasoning blend

1 teaspoon salt

Pinch ground pepper

2 tablespoons warm water (about 105 degrees F)

1 tablespoon agave nectar

1 teaspoon active dry yeast

½ cup unsweetened soy milk

4 teaspoons olive oil

¼ cup minced onion

Put the flour, vital wheat gluten, Italian seasoning blend, salt, and pepper in a medium bowl and stir to combine.

Put the water, agave nectar, and yeast in a small bowl and stir to combine. Set aside for about 5 minutes to proof; the yeast is ready when the mixture bubbles. Stir in the soy milk and 3 teaspoons of the oil. Pour into the flour mixture and stir well to form a dough.

Turn the dough out onto a lightly floured work surface and knead until smooth and cohesive, about 8 minutes. Knead in the onion, adding up to ¼ cup more flour, 1 tablespoon at a time, if needed to maintain a silky texture. Form the dough into a ball.

Lightly oil a medium bowl with olive oil. Put the dough in the bowl and turn to coat with the oil. Cover with a clean kitchen towel and let rise in a warm place until doubled in size, about 1½ hours (see Cook Smart).

Oil a 12-inch cast-iron skillet with olive oil. Transfer the dough to a lightly floured work surface and roll it out to an 11-inch round. Cut into 1-inch-wide strips and put the strips in the skillet with the sides touching. Brush the remaining teaspoon of oil evenly over the dough. Cover with the towel and let rise in a warm place until puffy but not doubled in size, about 30 minutes.

Outdoor Method

Put a large cast-iron skillet upside down on an outdoor grill to slightly elevate the skillet containing the breadsticks. Preheat the grill to medium heat.

Put the skillet containing the breadsticks on top of the inverted skillet. Close the grill and cook until golden, 17 to 20 minutes. To serve, pull the breadsticks apart. Serve hot or at room temperature.

Indoor Method

Preheat the oven to 375 degrees F. Bake the breadsticks in the skillet for 25 to 30 minutes, until golden.

Per serving: 182 calories, 6 g protein, 4 g fat (1 g sat), 31 g carbs, 466 mg sodium, 33 mg calcium, 2 g fiber

Cook Smart

- Savvy bakers employ the finger method to determine whether dough has doubled. To use this test, insert the tip of a finger, up to the first knuckle, into the dough. If the dough doesn't fill in after you remove your finger, it has doubled.

These stacks are eye-catching on an appetizer table and taste even better than they look. Habanero chiles make a double appearance in this recipe, in the marinade and in Habanero Lava. The chiles are quite spicy, but their flavor profile also includes citrus and floral notes that add nuances to this dish.

POLENTA STACKS

Yield: 16 stacks, 4 servings ● *Advance prep: Press the tofu and then marinate it for at least 1 hour. Make Habanero Marinade (page 163) and Habanero Lava (page 167).*

½ cup Habanero Marinade (page 163)

1 pound extra-firm tofu, pressed (see page 14)

1 (1-pound) tube polenta, cut into 16 rounds

1 tablespoon olive oil

1 tablespoon vegan mayonnaise

1 tablespoon vegan sour cream

½ teaspoon Habanero Lava (page 167)

Pinch salt

Pinch ground pepper

16 slices tomatoes, about ½ inch thick

1 tablespoon minced fresh cilantro

Pour the marinade into a 13 x 9-inch nonreactive baking pan. Cut the tofu in half lengthwise, then cut it crosswise seven times to form 16 somewhat square pieces. Put the tofu in the marinade and turn to coat. Cover and refrigerate for 1 hour or up to 3 days, turning the tofu occasionally.

Preheat a grill, grill pan, or electric grill to medium-high heat. If using an outdoor grill, line it with foil first.

Lightly mist the grill (and foil, if using) with cooking spray. Brush one side of the polenta rounds with about half of the oil. Put them on the grill oil-side down and cook until marked, about 4 minutes. Brush the remaining oil over the top of the rounds. Turn over and cook until the other side is marked, about 4 minutes. (If using an electric grill, keep it open for both the polenta and the tofu, and cook a few minutes longer if necessary.) Transfer to a baking sheet or a couple of plates.

Put the tofu on the grill, reserving the marinade. Cook until marked, about 5 minutes, occasionally basting with the marinade. Turn over and cook in the same fashion until the other side is marked, about 5 minutes.

Put the vegan mayonnaise, vegan sour cream, Habanero Lava, salt, and pepper in a small bowl and stir to combine.

Arrange the tomato slices on a serving platter. Top each with a polenta round and a tofu square. Drizzle the vegan mayonnaise mixture over the tofu, using a scant ½ teaspoon of the mixture for each stack. Sprinkle with the cilantro. Serve warm or at room temperature.

Per serving: 453 calories, 24 g protein, 17 g fat (3 g sat), 44 g carbs, 377 mg sodium, 327 mg calcium, 4 g fiber

More savory than sweet, these sausages, which are slightly denser than most homemade vegan sausages, can be used in a variety of ways: atop a pizza, in soup or chili, or in a sandwich. For extra kick, increase the amount of hot sauce.

SAUSAGE BITES

Yield: 2 sausages, 4 servings • Advance prep: Make Smoke Booster (page 161).

1 cup vital wheat gluten

¼ cup quick-cooking rolled oats

1 tablespoon chickpea flour

1 tablespoon nutritional yeast flakes

2 teaspoons onion powder

1 teaspoon ground fennel seeds

½ teaspoon dried marjoram

½ teaspoon red pepper flakes

½ teaspoon ground white pepper

½ teaspoon salt

½ teaspoon dried thyme

½ cup Smoke Booster (page 161)

¼ cup apple butter

1 tablespoon maple syrup

1 teaspoon hot sauce

1 to 2 tablespoons water or salt-free vegetable broth, if needed

Prepared yellow mustard, for dipping

Put the vital wheat gluten, oats, chickpea flour, nutritional yeast, onion powder, fennel, marjoram, red pepper flakes, white pepper, salt, and thyme in a medium bowl and stir to combine.

Put the Smoke Booster, apple butter, maple syrup, and hot sauce in a small bowl and stir until well combined. Pour into the vital wheat gluten mixture. Knead to form a ball of dough. If the mixture seems dry, add a little water, 1 tablespoon at a time, until the dough holds together. Divide the dough into 2 equal pieces.

Tear off two 12-inch pieces of foil. Put half of the sausage mixture on each piece of foil, forming it into a roughly cylindrical shape about 4 inches long. Roll up each piece in the foil, twisting the ends to secure. Steam the sausages for 50 minutes.

Let cool, then unwrap. The sausages can be used immediately or may be stored in a covered container or ziplock bag in the refrigerator for up to 1 week or in the freezer for up to 3 months.

Preheat a grill, grill pan, or electric grill to medium heat.

Lightly oil the grill with canola oil. Put the vegan sausages on the grill and cook, turning occasionally, until lightly browned, about 6 minutes. (If using an electric grill, keep it open and cook a few minutes longer if necessary.)

Cut the sausages into 1-inch-thick rounds and serve with yellow mustard for dipping.

Per serving: 217 calories, 25 g protein, 1 g fat (0.1 g sat), 25 g carbs, 380 mg sodium, 58 mg calcium, 3 g fiber

Note: Analysis doesn't include prepared yellow mustard for dipping.

SAUSAGE SANDWICHES: Don't slice the sausages after grilling. Leave them whole and serve them on buns with grilled onions and roasted peppers (see page 14).

Seitan shines when accented with Asian seasonings, and because of its meaty texture, it can stand up to grilling. The undercurrent of peanut butter is just enough to round out the spices. Feel free to boost the amount of red pepper flakes to suit your taste.

SEITAN SATAY

Yield: *4 skewers, 4 servings* ● Advance prep: *Make Seitan Roasts (page 90).*

½ cup minced scallions

⅓ cup apple juice

¼ cup salt-free
   vegetable broth

2 tablespoons reduced-
   sodium tamari

3 cloves garlic, minced

1 tablespoon toasted sesame
   oil

1 tablespoon ume plum
   vinegar

½ teaspoon red pepper flakes

¼ teaspoon ground pepper

12 ounces Seitan Roasts
   (page 90), cut into ¼- to
   ½-inch-thick slices

1 tablespoon smooth
   peanut butter

Put the scallions, apple juice, broth, tamari, garlic, oil, vinegar, red pepper flakes, and pepper in an 11 x 7-inch nonreactive baking pan and stir to combine. Add the seitan and turn to coat. Cover and refrigerate for 30 minutes or up to 3 days, turning the seitan occasionally.

About 30 minutes before you start grilling, soak four wooden skewers in water for 30 minutes. Alternatively, mist four metal skewers with cooking spray.

Remove the seitan from the marinade, reserving the marinade. Thread the seitan on the prepared skewers, piercing both ends of each piece to create a U shape; this will provide more surface to grill.

Preheat a grill, grill pan, or electric grill to medium-high heat.

Strain the marinade, reserving both the liquid and the solids. Set aside 2 tablespoons of the marinade for basting the seitan while cooking. Put the remaining marinade and the solids in a small grill-safe saucepan. Add the peanut butter and whisk to make a sauce.

Lightly oil the grill with canola oil. Put the skewers on the grill and cook until marked, about 4 minutes, basting them occasionally with the strained marinade. Turn over and cook in the same fashion until the other side is marked, about 3 minutes. (If using an electric grill, keep it open and cook a few minutes longer if necessary.)

Heat the sauce on an outdoor grill or on the stove over medium-low heat until just steaming, about 4 minutes. Serve the skewers with the sauce on the side for dipping or pass the sauce at the table.

Per serving: 237 calories, 27 g protein, 5 g fat (2 g sat), 17 g carbs, 1,310 mg sodium, 15 mg calcium, 1 g fiber

The inspiration behind these tempting bites is the well-known Vietnamese banh mi sandwich. Vegan banh mi sandwiches feature different proteins, such as tofu or seitan, and are almost always topped with crisp cucumbers and a seasoned sauce. This fun appetizer on a toothpick capitalizes on those flavors. You'll need about thirty toothpicks for serving.

SEITAN AND CUCUMBER MINIS

Yield: 8 servings ● *Advance prep: Make Seitan Ribz (page 94) and Sweet-and-Spicy Marinade (page 162).*

Dipping Sauce

3 tablespoons vegan mayonnaise

1 tablespoon reduced-sodium tamari

2 teaspoons sriracha sauce

1 teaspoon seasoned rice vinegar

1/8 teaspoon ground white pepper

Seasoned Seitan

12 ounces Seitan Ribz (page 94), grilled and cut into 30 cubes, about ¾ inch

1 cup Sweet-and-Spicy Marinade (page 162)

1 teaspoon peanut oil

Accompaniments

3 scallions, cut crosswise into 30 pieces, about 1 inch long

30 slices peeled cucumber, about ¼ inch thick

Fresh cilantro leaves, torn (optional)

1 teaspoon toasted sesame seeds, for garnish

To make the dipping sauce, put all the ingredients in a small bowl and whisk to combine. The sauce can be used immediately or may be stored in a covered container in the refrigerator for up to 1 week.

To prepare the seitan, put the ribz and marinade in a medium bowl and stir to coat. Heat the oil in a large cast-iron skillet on a grill over medium heat or on a stove over medium-high heat. Transfer the seitan to the skillet with a slotted spoon, reserving the marinade, and cook until browned all over, about 4 minutes, turning as needed. Pour in the marinade and stir until the seitan is evenly coated. Cook, stirring occasionally, until the marinade is absorbed, about 6 minutes.

To assemble the minis, have thirty toothpicks ready. Thread 1 piece of scallion, 1 seitan cube, 1 slice of cucumber, and 1 piece of optional cilantro on a toothpick. Thread the rest of the toothpicks in the same fashion. Arrange on a platter and garnish with the sesame seeds. Serve hot or at room temperature, with the dipping sauce on the side.

Per serving: 145 calories, 12 g protein, 5 g fat (0.4 g sat), 9 g carbs, 447 mg sodium, 38 mg calcium, 1 g fiber

Note: Analysis doesn't include cilantro leaves.

The hardest part of making this recipe is choosing what type of lettuce to use. Some people prefer butter lettuce because it's flexible and remains intact as a wrapping, making for appetizers that are easier to eat out of hand. Others prefer iceberg lettuce, which is prone to tearing but has a tantalizing crunch. Whatever lettuce you use, these appetizers are sure to be a hit, thanks to the savory grilled seitan and crisp vegetables.

LETTUCE WRAPS

Yield: 4 servings ● *Advance prep: Make Asian Spiced Cutlets (page 93).*

1 cup peeled and diced
  cucumber

3 tablespoons diced carrot

1 tablespoon minced red
  onion

1 tablespoon minced fresh
  cilantro (optional)

1½ teaspoons seasoned rice
  vinegar, plus more if desired

1 tablespoon hoisin sauce

½ teaspoon mirin, plus more if
  desired

½ teaspoon toasted sesame oil

½ teaspoon reduced-sodium
  tamari, plus more if desired

¼ teaspoon toasted sesame
  seeds

¼ teaspoon salt

Pinch ground white pepper

2 Asian Spiced Cutlets
  (page 93; also see Cook
  Smart), grilled

8 lettuce leaves

¾ cup mung bean sprouts

Sriracha sauce, for serving

Put the cucumber, carrot, onion, optional cilantro, and ½ teaspoon of the vinegar in a medium bowl and stir to combine.

Put the remaining teaspoon of vinegar and the hoisin sauce, mirin, oil, tamari, sesame seeds, salt, and white pepper in a medium bowl and whisk to combine. Taste and add more mirin, tamari, or vinegar if desired.

If the cutlets aren't hot, heat them on the grill or in a skillet over medium heat for 4 to 5 minutes. Slice the cutlets into thin strips. Put them in the bowl with the hoisin mixture. Toss until evenly coated.

Arrange the lettuce leaves on four plates. Divide the seitan strips evenly among the lettuce leaves and top with the vegetable mixture and the bean sprouts, dividing them evenly. To eat, wrap the leaf around the filling and eat like a handheld burrito. Serve with sriracha sauce on the side.

Per serving: 138 calories, 11 g protein, 4 g fat (1 g sat), 13 g carbs, 574 mg sodium, 61 mg calcium, 2 g fiber

Note: Analysis doesn't include sriracha sauce for serving.

Cook Smart

• You can substitute Seitan Roasts (page 90), cut into ½-inch-thick slices, for the Asian Spiced Cutlets.

Grilled Baby Artichokes, p. 22

Serve this fruity, light cocktail on the rocks or straight up. Grilling the fruit is key here. Not only does it add nuances to the flavor, it also substantially increases the amount of juice you'll get from the citrus.

SPARKLING MARGARITAS

Yield: 4 servings

2 lemons

2 limes

1 orange

1½ cups vegan Prosecco (see Cook Smart), chilled

½ cup vegan white tequila (see Cook Smart), chilled

2 tablespoons agave nectar, plus more if desired

Preheat a grill, grill pan, or electric grill to medium-high heat.

Slice the lemons, limes, and orange in half, put them on the grill cut-side down, and cook until marked, about 5 minutes. (If using an electric grill, keep it open and cook a few minutes longer if necessary.)

When the fruits are cool enough to handle, squeeze them and put the juice in a pitcher.

Add the Prosecco, tequila, and agave nectar and stir gently to combine. Taste and add up to 1 more tablespoon of agave nectar if desired. Serve chilled or over ice.

Per serving: 191 calories, 0 g protein, 0.1 g fat (0 g sat), 19 g carbs, 1 mg sodium, 22 mg calcium, 2 g fiber

Cook Smart

- For a nonalcoholic beverage, substitute sparkling water for the Prosecco and omit the tequila.
- It might come as a surprise that beer, wine, and spirits sometimes aren't vegan, generally because animal products are used in processing. For reliable information on vegan spirits, visit barnivore.com.

Chapter 3

Sensational Soups
and Sandwiches

Cold soups are a delightful way to start a meal, piquing the palate for courses to follow. They also make great picnic fare. In this recipe, gazpacho, which is always a delightfully fresh-tasting soup, is enhanced with roasted bell peppers and sweet corn.

RED BELL PEPPER GAZPACHO

Yield: 4 servings ● *Advance prep: Make Avocado Sauce (page 173).*

2½ cups tomato juice

1½ cups peeled, seeded, and chopped cucumber

2 roasted red bell peppers (see page 14), coarsely chopped

½ cup corn kernels, cut from a cooked cob or Roasted Corn on the Cob (page 130; also see Cook Smart)

½ cup minced red onion

3 tablespoons cider vinegar

2 tablespoons chopped celery

Juice from ½ lemon

½ teaspoon ground coriander

½ teaspoon salt

¼ teaspoon ground pepper

¼ cup Avocado Sauce (page 173), for garnish

1 tablespoon minced fresh mint, for garnish

Put the tomato juice, ½ cup of the cucumber, and the bell peppers in a blender and process until smooth.

Pour into a large bowl. Stir in the remaining cucumber and the corn, onion, vinegar, celery, lemon juice, coriander, salt, and pepper. Cover and refrigerate for at least 3 hours to allow the flavors to meld. After it has chilled, the soup can be served or stored in a covered container in the refrigerator for up to 3 days.

Serve garnished with the Avocado Sauce and mint.

Per serving: 90 calories, 3 g protein, 0.3 g fat (0.0 g sat), 19 g carbs, 593 mg sodium, 75 mg calcium, 4 g fiber

Note: Analysis doesn't include Avocado Sauce for serving.

Cook Smart

• If fresh corn is out of season, use frozen corn kernels. Put the corn in a dry cast-iron skillet over medium-high heat and cook, stirring occasionally, until browned, about 8 minutes.

SPICY RED BELL PEPPER GAZPACHO: If you prefer a spicier soup, add a roasted and seeded jalapeño chile (see page 14) along with the bell peppers; the chile need not be peeled.

Ramen on the grill? You bet! Surprise your family or guests with this unusual twist on the noodle favorite. To make the soup a more filling meal, top each bowl with an Asian Spiced Cutlet (page 93) sliced into strips.

ASIAN STREET SOUP

Yield: 4 servings

1 small red onion, cut in half
   and sliced into half-moons

1 cup sugar snap peas, trimmed

1 Thai chile, seeded
   and thinly sliced

3 cloves garlic, sliced

2 teaspoons toasted sesame oil

1 teaspoon grated fresh ginger

2¼ cups salt-free
   vegetable broth

Noodles from 2 packages
   (2 ounces each) ramen

Seasoning packets from
   the ramen (optional;
   see Cook Smart)

2 cups chopped baby bok choy

2 tablespoons minced fresh
   Thai or Italian basil

2 tablespoons mirin

1 tablespoon reduced-
   sodium tamari

1 tablespoon seasoned
   rice vinegar

1 teaspoon sambal oelek
   (see Cook Smart)

½ teaspoon dark miso

Salt (optional)

Ground pepper (optional)

Outdoor Method

Preheat an outdoor grill to medium-high heat.

Put the onion, sugar snap peas, chile, garlic, oil, and ginger in a 10-inch square foil roasting pan and stir until the vegetables are evenly coated with the oil. Put the pan on the grill and close the lid. Cook, opening the grill and stirring occasionally, until the vegetables are fragrant, about 3 minutes. Stir in the broth. Add the ramen noodles, breaking them apart as you put them in, and the optional seasoning packets. Stir in the bok choy. Close the lid and cook, stirring occasionally, until the noodles are tender, about 12 minutes.

Put the basil, mirin, tamari, vinegar, sambal oelek, and miso in a small bowl and stir to combine. Take the ramen off the grill and stir in the basil mixture. Season with salt and pepper to taste if desired.

Indoor Method

Make the soup on the stove in a large soup pot over medium heat, preparing it as directed through the addition of the ramen noodles and bok choy. Decrease the heat to medium-low and cook, stirring occasionally, for only about 3 minutes, until the ramen is tender. Season the soup as directed.

Per serving: 225 calories, 5 g protein, 8 g fat (3 g sat), 33 g carbs, 499 mg sodium, 35 mg calcium, 3 g fiber

Cook Smart

- Be sure to read the ramen packages to make sure the seasoning packets are vegan. If they aren't, just omit them from the soup.
- Sambal oelek is a concentrated paste made from chiles, salt, oil, and vinegar. Look for it at Asian markets or in the Asian section of well-stocked supermarkets. For a spicier soup, add more sambal oelek as desired.

A generous amount of white wine adds depth and richness to this chowder, while the grilled vegetables give it wonderful body. It freezes well too, providing a happy reminder of the best of summer's produce in other seasons.

ROASTED CORN CHOWDER

Yield: 6 servings ● Advance prep: Make Roasted Corn on the Cob (page 130) and Barbeque Sauce in a Flash (page 165).

2 leeks, white part only, washed well (see Cook Smart, page 29) and cut in half lengthwise

3 red potatoes, scrubbed and cubed

½ red bell pepper, diced

½ cup diced celery

1 tablespoon olive oil

3 cloves garlic, peeled

1 teaspoon smoked paprika

1 teaspoon dried rosemary

½ teaspoon ground pepper

1½ cups dry white wine or salt-free vegetable broth

2 cups salt-free vegetable broth

Outdoor Method

Preheat an outdoor grill to medium-high heat.

Put the leeks, potatoes, bell pepper, celery, oil, garlic, paprika, rosemary, and pepper in a deep 13 x 9-inch foil roasting pan. Stir until the vegetables are evenly coated with the oil and spices. Put the pan on the grill and cook, stirring occasionally, until fragrant, about 3 minutes. Decrease the heat to medium-low and stir in the wine. Cook, stirring occasionally, until the vegetables are tender, about 20 minutes.

Put the vegetables and any liquid in the pan in a food processor. Add the broth and lemon juice and process until smooth. Add the corn and pulse a few times; some of the corn should remain in kernels, so don't process until smooth. Transfer to a large saucepan and heat on the grill over medium-low heat, stirring occasionally, until steaming, about 10 minutes. Ladle the chowder into four bowls. Drizzle each serving with 1 tablespoon of the barbecue sauce.

Juice from ½ lemon

1 cup corn kernels cut
from Roasted Corn on
the Cob (page 130; also
see Cook Smart)

¼ cup Barbecue Sauce in
a Flash (page 165)

Indoor Method

Preheat the oven to 500 degrees F. Put the leeks, potatoes, bell pepper, celery, oil, garlic, paprika, rosemary, and pepper in a deep 13 x 9-inch nonreactive baking pan and stir until the vegetables are evenly coated. Bake for 10 minutes, add the wine, stir, and bake for about 10 minutes longer, until the vegetables are tender. Process, heat, and serve as directed.

Per serving: 199 calories, 4 g protein, 3 g fat (0.4 g sat), 31 g carbs, 401 mg sodium, 34 mg calcium, 3 g fiber

Cook Smart

• Frozen corn can also be used. Put the corn in a dry cast-iron skillet over medium-high heat and cook, stirring occasionally, until browned, about 8 minutes.

Although green chimichurri sauce from Argentina is more widely known, the red version used in this sandwich deserves a place in your kitchen. The spice in the sauce is offset by a cabbage slaw accented with fresh lime juice, making this wrap a winner.

CHIMICHURRI WRAPS

Yield: 4 wraps ● *Advance prep: Make Seitan Roasts (page 90) and Red-Hot Chimichurri Sauce (page 168).*

Cabbage-Cucumber Slaw

2 scallions

4 cups shredded
  green cabbage

¾ cup peeled and
  diced cucumber

1 carrot, shredded

2 tablespoons red
  wine vinegar

Juice from ½ lime

1 tablespoon agave nectar

Pinch ground pepper

1 to 2 tablespoons minced
  jalapeño chile (optional)

Seitan and Accompaniments

1 pound Seitan Roasts (page
  90), cut into
  ¼-inch-thick slices

½ cup Red-Hot Chimichurri
  Sauce (page 168)

2 tablespoons vegan
  mayonnaise

4 (8-inch) flour tortillas,
  warmed (see Cook Smart)

To make the slaw, preheat a grill, grill pan, or electric grill to medium heat.

Lightly oil the grill with canola oil. Put the scallions on the grill and cook until marked, about 4 minutes. (If using an electric grill, keep it open and cook a few minutes longer if necessary.)

When the scallions are cool enough to handle, trim and chop them. Put the scallions in a medium bowl. Add the cabbage, cucumber, carrot, vinegar, lime juice, agave nectar, and pepper and stir to combine. Add the optional chile to taste and mix well.

To prepare the seitan, put the slices on the grill and cook until marked, about 4 minutes. Turn over and cook until the other side is marked, about 3 minutes. (If using an electric grill, keep it open and cook a few minutes longer if necessary.)

When the seitan is cool enough to handle, cut it into ½-inch-wide strips. Put the seitan and sauce in a large cast-iron skillet. Put the skillet on an outdoor grill or on the stove over medium heat. Cook, stirring occasionally, until steaming, about 4 minutes.

To assemble the wraps, spread the vegan mayonnaise evenly over the tortillas. Divide the seitan, sauce, and slaw evenly among the tortillas. Fold in the sides and roll up to enclose the filling. Cut in half to serve.

Per wrap: 454 calories, 40 g protein, 9 g fat (1 g sat), 48 g carbs, 847 mg sodium, 944 mg calcium, 3 g fiber

Cook Smart

• To warm the tortillas, preheat the oven to 350 degrees F. Wrap the tortillas in foil and bake for 10 minutes. Alternatively, put the foil-wrapped tortillas on an outdoor grill over medium heat for 8 to 10 minutes, until heated through, turning the packet over halfway through the cooking time.

Originating in Buffalo, New York, Buffalo wings remain a perennial favorite. Happily, vegans have adopted the addictive hot sauce that makes Buffalo wings distinctive, smothering every plant-based protein and a variety of other foods in it. Here, grilled smoked tofu is slathered with a cashew-based version of the sauce and paired with crunchy fresh vegetables to create a sandwich that saves you having to shuffle off to Buffalo.

SMOKY BUFFALO TOFU WRAPS

Yield: 4 wraps ● Advance prep: Soak the cashews for 1 hour. Make Smoke Booster (page 161).

Buffalo Sauce

⅓ cup cashews, soaked in cold water for 1 hour and drained

2 tablespoons hot sauce

2 tablespoons unsweetened soy milk

1 tablespoon Smoke Booster (page 161)

1 teaspoon prepared yellow mustard

⅛ teaspoon ground pepper

Salt (optional)

Tofu and Accompaniments

1 pound smoked tofu, homemade (page 87 or 88) or store-bought

¼ cup minced celery

¼ cup minced red onion

1 tablespoon sweet pickle relish

4 (8-inch) flour tortillas, warmed (see Cook Smart, page 52)

1 (6-inch) cucumber, peeled and cut into ¼-inch-thick rounds

2 cups arugula, lightly packed

To make the sauce, put all the ingredients in a small blender or food processor and process until smooth. Season with salt to taste if desired. The sauce can be used immediately or may be stored in a covered container in the refrigerator for up to 5 days.

To prepare the tofu, preheat a grill, grill pan, or electric grill to medium-high heat.

Lightly oil the grill with canola oil. Put the tofu on the grill and cook until marked, about 5 minutes. Turn over and cook until the other side is marked, about 5 minutes. (If using an electric grill, keep it open and cook a few minutes longer if necessary.)

When the tofu is cool enough to handle, dice it and put it in a medium bowl. Add the sauce, celery, onion, and sweet pickle relish and stir to combine.

To assemble the wraps, divide the tofu mixture evenly among the tortillas. Top with the cucumber and arugula. Fold in the sides and roll up to enclose the filling. Cut in half to serve.

Per wrap: 380 calories, 23 g protein, 19 g fat (4 g sat), 32 g carbs, 824 mg sodium, 178 mg calcium, 3 g fiber

Cook Smart

- This wrap is easy to transport. Pack the parts separately and assemble the sandwich at mealtime.

Teppanyaki is a Japanese cuisine prepared on a smooth cooking surface that's so hot it results in a grilled flavor. When the food is actually cooked on a grill, the flavor is even deeper. Here, seitan dressed with a zippy sauce and tempered with fresh basil leaves is rolled up in tortillas, and then the wraps are grilled until lightly toasted. Dipping them enhances the fun factor. Give it a try and see if you don't agree.

TEPPANYAKI SEITAN WRAPS

Yield: 4 wraps • Advance prep: Make Seitan Ribz (page 94) and Sweet-and-Spicy Marinade (page 162).

4 scallions

2 tablespoons vegan mayonnaise

2 teaspoons sriracha sauce, plus more as needed

4 (10-inch) flour tortillas, warmed (see Cook Smart, page 52)

1 pound Seitan Ribz (page 94), thinly sliced

30 to 40 fresh basil leaves

¾ cup Sweet-and-Spicy Marinade (page 162), heated until steaming

Preheat a grill, grill pan, or electric grill to medium heat.

Lightly oil the grill with canola oil. Put the scallions on the grill and cook until marked, about 4 minutes. (If using an electric grill, keep it open and cook a few minutes longer if necessary.)

When the scallions are cool enough to handle, trim and chop them.

Put the vegan mayonnaise and sriracha sauce in a small bowl and whisk to combine. Taste and add more sriracha sauce if desired. Spread 1½ teaspoons of the mixture across the center of each tortilla, leaving about 1 inch uncoated on the perimeter. Divide the seitan and scallions evenly among the tortillas. Top with the basil leaves. Fold in the sides and roll up to enclose the filling.

Outdoor Grill or Grill Pan Method

Put the wraps on the outdoor grill or grill pan seam-side down. Put a baking sheet on top of the wraps and weigh the baking sheet down with a cast-iron skillet. If using an outdoor grill, close the lid. Cook until marked, 2 to 3 minutes. Turn over and cook in the same fashion until the other side is marked, 2 to 3 minutes. Serve the wraps with the marinade on the side for dipping.

Electric Grill Method

Increase the heat of the electric grill to medium-high. Put the wraps on the grill seam-side down, close the lid, and cook until marked, about 5 minutes. Serve as directed.

Per wrap: 561 calories, 38 g protein, 14 g fat (1 g sat), 66 g carbs, 1,360 mg sodium, 120 mg calcium, 3 g fiber

Leftover ratatouille brings great grill flavor to these simple-to-make sandwiches. The olive mayonnaise provides a salty accent to the subtly sweet grilled vegetables piled high on toasted French bread. Serve with a fork and knife—and lots of napkins.

OPEN-FACED RATATOUILLE SANDWICHES

Yield: 6 sandwiches ● Advance prep: Make Grilled Ratatouille (page 132).

¼ cup vegan mayonnaise

¼ cup chopped kalamata olives

1 tablespoon nutritional yeast flakes

1 (12-inch) loaf French bread, cut in half horizontally and grilled

12 lettuce leaves

2 cups Grilled Ratatouille (page 132), at room temperature

Put the vegan mayonnaise, olives, and nutritional yeast in a small blender and process until smooth. The mixture can be used immediately or may be stored in a covered container in the refrigerator for up to 3 days.

Spread the mayonnaise mixture on the cut sides of the bread. Top with the lettuce and ratatouille. Cut in half crosswise and serve open-faced.

Per sandwich: 304 calories, 7 g protein, 10 g fat (1 g sat), 39 g carbs, 611 mg sodium, 23 mg calcium, 10 g fiber

Cook Smart

- For a picnic sandwich, don't toast the bread. Package the parts separately, keeping the spread cool, and assemble when you're ready to eat.

Built on a base of Rosemary Flatbread, this sandwich is piled high with glazed grilled vegetables and a refreshing arugula salad. Resist the urge to pour any remaining dressing over the sandwiches after stacking, as it could make the bread soggy. Serve with plenty of napkins. Note that, for this recipe, the flatbread dough must be divided in half before shaping and grilling or baking.

THE VEG WEDGE

Yield: 1 sandwich, 6 servings
Advance prep: Make Rosemary Flatbread (page 36) and Deviled Spread (page 31).

Vegetables

2 tablespoons olive oil

Pinch ground pepper

4 portobello mushrooms, stems and gills removed

8 ounces eggplant, cut lengthwise into ½-inch-thick slabs

1 red bell pepper, cut into ½-inch-thick rings

3 slices onion, about ½ inch thick

To prepare the vegetables, preheat a grill, grill pan, or electric grill to medium-high heat.

Lightly oil the grill with canola oil. Put the olive oil and pepper in a small bowl and stir to combine. Brush about half the mixture evenly over the mushrooms, eggplant, bell pepper, and onion. Put the vegetables on the grill oiled-side down and cook until marked, about 5 minutes. Brush the remaining oil mixture over the vegetables. Turn over and cook until the eggplant and the center of the mushrooms are tender, about 5 minutes. (If using an electric grill, keep it open and cook a few minutes longer if necessary.) Decrease the grill heat to medium.

When the vegetables are cool enough to handle, cut the mushrooms and eggplant into ½-inch-wide strips. Cut the pepper rings in half. Cut the onion slices in half and separate the layers. Put the vegetables in a medium bowl.

To make the glaze, put all the ingredients in a small bowl and stir to combine. Pour over the vegetables and toss to coat.

To make the salad, put the arugula in a medium bowl. Drizzle with the vinegar and tamari and toss to coat.

Outdoor Grill, Grill Pan, or Stovetop Method

To assemble and cook the sandwich, tear off one 24-inch piece of foil. Put 1 flatbread on the foil. Top with the spread, distributing it evenly. Spoon the grilled vegetables evenly over the spread and top with the salad. Put the second flatbread on top and press down gently but firmly. Wrap tightly in the foil.

Glaze

1 teaspoon hot sauce

1 teaspoon maple syrup

1 tablespoon reduced-
sodium tamari

1 teaspoon rice vinegar

Pinch ground pepper

Salad

4 cups arugula, lightly packed

1½ teaspoons balsamic vinegar

1½ teaspoons reduced-
sodium tamari

Bread and Spread

Rosemary Flatbread (page 36),
made into 2 (6- to 7-inch)
rounds, grilled or baked

1 cup Deviled Spread (page 31)

Decrease the heat to medium. Put the wrapped sandwich on the grill or grill pan and put a skillet on top of the sandwich to press it. Cook for about 10 minutes, until warmed through, turning once halfway through the cooking time. To serve, unwrap the sandwich and cut it into wedges.

Electric Grill Method

To assemble and cook the sandwich, layer the ingredients on the flatbread in the same way, but omit the foil. Decrease the heat to medium and put the unwrapped sandwich on the grill. Close the lid and cook for about 10 minutes, until warmed through, without turning the sandwich.

Per serving: 291 calories, 14 g protein, 14 g fat (1 g sat), 29 g carbs, 793 mg sodium, 58 mg calcium, 4 g fiber

Cook Smart

• The wrapped sandwiches can also be warmed, one at a time, in a cast-iron skillet preheated over medium-high heat. Just put a second skillet on top to press the sandwich, and cook as directed.

For these simple, savory sandwiches, tofu is steeped in a marinade with distinctive Italian seasonings, grilled, and then nestled in ciabatta rolls along with a light red bell pepper spread and crisp romaine lettuce.

ITALIAN TOFU SANDWICHES

Yield: 4 sandwiches • *Advance prep: Make Tofu Italiano (page 84).*

Bell Pepper Mayo

¼ cup coarsely chopped
  roasted red bell pepper
  (see page 14)

3 tablespoons vegan
  mayonnaise

2 cloves garlic, minced

1 teaspoon capers

Pinch ground pepper

Tofu and Accompaniments

4 ciabatta rolls, split

1 pound Tofu Italiano (page 84),
  marinated but not grilled

4 thin slices red onion,
  separated into rings

8 romaine lettuce leaves

To make the bell pepper mayo, put all the ingredients in a small blender and process until smooth. The spread can be used immediately or may be stored in a covered container in the refrigerator for up to 1 week.

To grill the rolls and tofu and assemble the sandwiches, preheat a grill, grill pan, or electric grill to medium-high heat.

Put the rolls on the grill, cut-side down. Pressing with a turner occasionally, cook until marked, about 4 minutes. (If using an electric grill, keep it open for both the rolls and the tofu and cook a few minutes longer if necessary.)

Lightly oil the grill with canola oil. Put the tofu on the grill, reserving the marinade. Cook until marked, about 5 minutes, while occasionally basting with the marinade. Turn over and cook in the same fashion until the other side is marked, about 5 minutes.

Spread the mayo evenly on the cut sides of the rolls. Put the tofu on the bottom halves of the rolls. Cover with the onion, lettuce, and top halves of the rolls.

Per sandwich: 502 calories, 27 g protein, 20 g fat (3 g sat), 55 g carbs, 621 mg sodium, 158 mg calcium, 3 g fiber

Jalapeño chiles and beer are a natural combination in this marinade. If vegan Mexican ale is available, use it here to complement the other seasonings.

MEXICAN SEITAN SANDWICHES

Yield: 4 sandwiches • Advance prep: Make Classic Cutlets (page 91) and Mexican Slaw (page 123). Marinate the cutlets for at least 1 hour.

Mexican Cutlets

½ cup vegan ale (see Cook Smart)

2 teaspoons agave nectar

1 teaspoon olive oil

1 clove garlic, minced

½ teaspoon ground white pepper

4 Classic Cutlets (page 91)

Accompaniments

1 avocado, chopped

½ jalapeño chile, seeded and minced

Salt (optional)

Ground pepper (optional)

4 crusty French rolls, split and grilled

2 cups Mexican Slaw (page 123)

To prepare the cutlets, put the ale, agave nectar, oil, garlic, and white pepper in an 11 x 7-inch nonreactive baking pan and stir to combine. Add the cutlets and turn to coat. Cover and refrigerate for 1 hour or up to 3 days, turning the cutlets occasionally.

Preheat a grill, grill pan, or electric grill to medium-high heat.

Lightly oil the grill with canola oil. Put the cutlets on the grill, reserving the marinade. If using an outdoor grill, close the lid. Cook until marked, about 4 minutes, while occasionally basting with the marinade. Turn over and cook in the same fashion until the other side is marked, about 3 minutes. (If using an electric grill, keep it open and cook a few minutes longer if necessary.)

When the cutlets are cool enough to handle, slice them into ½-inch-wide strips.

To assemble the sandwiches, put the avocado in a small bowl and mash it with a fork or potato masher. Stir in the chile. Season to taste with salt and pepper. Spread the mixture evenly on the cut sides of the rolls. Put the slices from 1 cutlet on the bottom half of each roll. Cover with ½ cup of the slaw and the top half of the roll.

Per sandwich: 447 calories, 28 g protein, 11 g fat (2 g sat), 50 g carbs, 401 mg sodium, 111 mg calcium, 8 g fiber

Cook Smart

• For a reliable list of vegan beers, visit barnivore.com. You can even search by country to find a vegan Mexican beer!

Tangy sauerkraut seasoned with caraway seeds partners perfectly with smoky grilled tofu and a thick slice of apple to make a very satisfying breakfast sandwich. Although this recipe was designed to start your day, it also makes a terrific lunch or dinner.

REUBEN-INSPIRED BREAKFAST SANDWICHES

Yield: 4 sandwiches ● Advance prep: Press the tofu and then marinate it for at least 8 hours. Make Russian Dressing with a Kick (page 177).

Tofu Corned Beef

⅓ cup pickle juice

2 tablespoons canola oil

2 tablespoons reduced-sodium tamari

2 teaspoons ground coriander

2 teaspoons ground cumin

2 teaspoons smoked paprika

1 teaspoon ground cardamom

2 pounds extra-firm tofu, pressed (see page 14) and cut in half laterally to make 4 slabs

To make the tofu corned beef, put the pickle juice, oil, tamari, coriander, cumin, paprika, and cardamom in a 13 x 9-inch nonreactive baking pan. Add the tofu and turn to coat. Cover and refrigerate for 8 hours or up to 3 days, turning the tofu occasionally.

Heat a grill, grill pan, or electric grill to medium heat.

Lightly mist the grill with cooking spray. Put the tofu on the grill, reserving the marinade. Cook until marked, about 4 minutes, occasionally basting with the marinade. Turn a quarter turn to get hatch marks and grill in the same fashion until marked, about 2 minutes. Turn the tofu over and cook the other side in the same fashion. (If using an electric grill, keep it open and cook a few minutes longer if necessary.)

When the tofu is cool enough to handle, use a biscuit cutter the same size as the English muffins to cut rounds from the tofu slabs. Reserve the tofu scraps for use in another dish.

To prepare the accompaniments, tear off one 18-inch piece of foil. Put the sauerkraut in the center of the foil and sprinkle the caraway seeds and pepper over it. If cooking on a grill pan or electric grill, drizzle the optional liquid smoke over the sauerkraut for a more flavorful sandwich. Wrap the foil around the sauerkraut and put the packet on the grill. Cook for 5 minutes, then turn over and cook for 5 minutes longer. Move the packet to a cooler part of the grill.

Put the apple rounds on the grill and cook until marked, 3 to 4 minutes. Turn a quarter turn to get hatch marks and cook until marked, about 2 minutes. Turn the rounds over and cook the other

Accompaniments

3 cups sauerkraut, drained

1 teaspoon caraway seeds

Pinch ground pepper

½ teaspoon liquid
  smoke (optional)

1 apple, cored and cut into
  4 rounds about ½ inch thick

4 English muffins, split

½ cup Russian Dressing
  with a Kick (page 177)

side in the same fashion. (If using an electric grill, keep it open for both the apples and the English muffins, and cook a few minutes longer if necessary.)

Put the English muffins on the grill cut-side down. Pressing with a turner occasionally, cook until marked, about 2 minutes.

To assemble the sandwiches, spread the dressing on the cut sides of the English muffins. Put the tofu rounds on the bottom halves of the English muffins. Cover with the apple slices, sauerkraut, and the top halves of the English muffins.

Per sandwich: 628 calories, 42 g protein, 32 g fat (6 g sat), 46 g carbs, 1,213 mg sodium, 356 mg calcium, 6 g fiber

The traditional flavors of a Reuben sandwich burst forth from a panini in this newfangled version of the classic. The tempeh is cut in half laterally to form thin slabs, enhancing its capacity to absorb the marinade. This recipe is best made indoors to allow the outside of the sandwiches to crisp without drying out the bread.

BLUSHIN' RUSSIAN TEMPEH PANINI

Yield: 4 sandwiches

2 tablespoons balsamic vinegar

1 teaspoon garam masala

1 teaspoon olive oil

8 ounces tempeh, poached (see page 14)

1 cup sauerkraut, squeezed dry (see Cook Smart)

½ cup minced celery

½ cup minced onion

¼ cup vegan mayonnaise

2 tablespoons minced dill pickle

1 tablespoon ketchup

2 teaspoon capers, drained

¼ teaspoon caraway seeds

¼ teaspoon smoked paprika

Pinch ground pepper

Put the vinegar, garam masala, and oil in an 11 x 7-inch nonreactive baking pan and stir to combine. Cut the tempeh in half crosswise, then cut each piece in half laterally to create 2 thinner slabs. Add the tempeh to the marinade and turn to coat. Cover and refrigerate until the marinade is absorbed, or up to 1 hour.

Preheat an electric grill to high heat or put a grill pan over high heat.

Lightly mist the grill or grill pan with cooking spray. If possible, open the electric grill flat. If not, leave the grill open and cook in batches if necessary. Put the tempeh on the grill or grill pan and cook until marked, about 5 minutes. Turn over and cook until the other side is marked, about 5 minutes.

When the tempeh is cool enough to handle, dice it and put it in a medium bowl. Add the sauerkraut, celery, onion, vegan mayonnaise, pickles, ketchup, capers, caraway seeds, paprika, and pepper and stir to combine.

Spread the margarine on one side of each piece of bread. Put 4 pieces of the bread on a piece of parchment paper, margarine-side down. Divide the tempeh mixture evenly among them, then top with the remaining 4 slices of the bread, margarine-side up.

Electric Grill Method

Carefully wipe the grill plates clean with a paper towel. Preheat the grill to high heat.

Transfer the sandwiches to the grill and close. Cook until marked and golden, about 5 minutes. Cut in half diagonally to serve.

2 tablespoons vegan
  margarine, softened

8 slices sandwich bread

Grill Pan Method

Clean the grill pan and put it over high heat. Put the sandwiches on the grill pan and put a baking sheet on top of them. Weigh the baking sheet down with a cast-iron skillet. Cook until golden on the bottom, about 3 minutes. Turn over and cook in the same fashion until the other side is golden, about 3 minutes. Serve as directed.

Per sandwich: 473 calories, 15 g protein, 24 g fat (4 g sat), 39 g carbs, 812 mg sodium, 383 mg calcium, 4 g fiber

Cook Smart

- You can use a salad spinner to remove excess moisture from the sauerkraut.

Daikon radishes, which look like large, white carrots, are similar to red radishes in flavor and texture, having a slightly spicy, earthy crunch. Here I've paired the two radishes in a crisp salad with Asian flavors. The slaw's texture plays well against the tender, juicy mushrooms, and there's just something irresistible about a cool topping on a hot sandwich.

TERIYAKI PORTOBELLO BURGERS

Yield: 4 sandwiches ● *Advance prep: Make Teriyaki Sauce (page 166). Marinate the mushrooms for 1 hour.*

Asian Slaw

1½ cups shredded
   Chinese cabbage

¾ cup shredded daikon radish

½ cup grated red radishes

3 tablespoons chopped
   scallions

2 tablespoons shredded carrot

1 tablespoon seasoned
   rice vinegar

1 teaspoon agave nectar

1 teaspoon grated fresh ginger

½ teaspoon toasted sesame oil

Mushrooms and Buns

1½ cups Teriyaki Sauce
   (page 166)

4 portobello mushrooms,
   stems and gills removed

4 burger buns, split and
   grilled if desired

To make the slaw, put all the ingredients in a medium bowl and stir until well combined. Cover and refrigerate for at least 1 hour to allow the flavors to meld. The slaw can be stored in a covered container in the refrigerator for up to 3 days.

To prepare the mushrooms, pour the sauce into a 13 x 9-inch baking pan. Add the mushrooms and turn to coat. Let marinate at room temperature for 1 hour.

Preheat a grill, grill pan, or electric grill to medium-high heat.

Lightly oil the grill with canola oil. Put the mushrooms on the grill stem-side up, reserving the marinade. Cook until marked, about 5 minutes. Turn over and cook until the other side is marked and the flesh is soft and tender in the center, about 5 minutes, basting with the reserved marinade during the last few minutes of cooking. (If using an electric grill, keep it open and cook a few minutes longer if necessary.)

Put the mushrooms on the bottom halves of the buns. Cover with the slaw and the top halves of the buns.

Per sandwich: 239 calories, 11 g protein, 5 g fat (1 g sat), 52 g carbs, 753 mg sodium, 13 mg calcium, 4 g fiber

The inspiration behind this recipe was an open jar of mango chutney lurking in the refrigerator. These aromatic sweet-and-sour burgers are sure to raise eyebrows and be a conversation starter, especially among meat eaters.

PORTOBELLO BURGERS
WITH MANGO CHUTNEY MARINADE

Yield: 4 sandwiches ● *Advance prep: Marinate the mushrooms for 1 hour.*

Chutney Sauce

¼ cup mango chutney

2 tablespoons vegan mayonnaise

2 teaspoons hot sauce

Mushrooms

1 cup salt-free vegetable broth

1/4 cup mango chutney

2 tablespoons minced red onion

1 tablespoon reduced-
    sodium tamari

1 tablespoon balsamic vinegar

2 cloves garlic, minced

1 teaspoon ground coriander

1 teaspoon toasted sesame oil

1/2 teaspoon ground white pepper

Pinch red pepper flakes

4 portobello mushrooms,
    stems and gills removed

Accompaniments

4 burger buns, split and
    grilled if desired

Sliced red onions

Sliced dill pickles

To make the sauce, put all the ingredients in a small blender and process until smooth. The sauce can be used immediately or may be stored in a covered container in the refrigerator for up to 5 days.

To prepare the mushrooms, put the broth, chutney, onion, tamari, vinegar, garlic, coriander, oil, white pepper, and red pepper flakes in a small saucepan and stir to combine. Bring to a boil over medium-high heat. Decrease the heat to low and simmer uncovered, stirring occasionally, for 10 minutes.

Put the mushrooms in a 13 x 9-inch nonreactive baking pan stem-side up. Pour the chutney mixture evenly over the mushrooms and let marinate at room temperature for 1 hour.

Preheat a grill, grill pan, or electric grill to medium-high heat.

Lightly oil the grill with canola oil. Put the mushrooms on the grill stem-side up, reserving the marinade. Cook until marked, about 5 minutes, occasionally basting with the marinade. Turn over and cook in the same fashion until the other side is marked and the flesh is soft and tender in the center, about 5 minutes. (If using an electric grill, keep it open and cook a few minutes longer if necessary.)

To assemble the burgers, spread the sauce evenly on the cut sides of the buns. Put the mushrooms on the bottom halves of the buns. Cover with the onions, pickles, and top halves of the buns.

Per sandwich: 250 calories, 9 g protein, 8 g fat (1 g sat), 49 g carbs, 612 mg sodium, 57 mg calcium, 3 g fiber

Note: Analysis doesn't include red onions and dill pickles for serving.

For the best texture, be sure to cook these burgers until the outside has a blackened, crispy crust. They take well to additional ingredients, such as chipotle chiles or different spices, so after you've tried the basic recipe, I encourage you to experiment.

BLACK BEAN BURGERS

Yield: 6 sandwiches • Advance prep: Soak the bulgur for 1 hour. Make Barbecue Sauce in a Flash (page 165).

½ cup boiling water

½ cup bulgur

1 (15-ounce) can black beans, drained and rinsed

1 cup chopped cremini mushrooms

½ cup cooked brown rice

½ cup minced onion

3 tablespoons Barbecue Sauce in a Flash (page 165)

2 cloves garlic, minced

2 teaspoons liquid smoke

1 teaspoon onion powder

½ teaspoon salt

½ teaspoon ground pepper

1⅓ cups vital wheat gluten

1 tablespoon olive oil

6 burger buns, split and grilled if desired

Favorite burger toppings, such as lettuce, tomato, pickles, and onion

Pour the water over the bulgur, cover, and let sit for 1 hour until all the liquid is absorbed.

Put the beans, mushrooms, rice, onion, barbecue sauce, garlic, liquid smoke, onion powder, salt, and pepper in a food processor and pulse to combine. Add the vital wheat gluten and process until the mixture pulls away from the work bowl and gluten threads are visible, 2 to 3 minutes. Transfer to a medium bowl. Add the bulgur and knead it into the mixture, pressing it in if necessary.

Tear off six 12-inch pieces of foil. Divide the mixture into 6 equal portions. Put each portion on a piece of foil and form into a patty about 3½ to 4 inches in diameter. Fold the foil around the patties but don't seal it tightly, as the patties will expand during steaming. Steam for 1 hour. Refrigerate before grilling for optimum texture. The patties may also be frozen after steaming (see Cook Smart).

Outdoor Method

Preheat an outdoor grill to medium heat. Put the oil in a large cast-iron skillet. Put the skillet on the grill and heat until the oil begins to ripple, about 3 minutes. Unwrap the patties and put them in the skillet. Cook until blackened, about 5 minutes. Turn over and cook until the other side is blackened, about 5 minutes.

Put the patties on the bottom halves of the buns. Cover with other toppings as desired and the top halves of the buns.

Indoor Method

Cook the patties in a skillet on the stove as directed. Alternatively, use an electric grill fitted with the smooth plates and preheated to high heat. Lightly mist the grill with cooking spray. Unwrap the patties and cook with the lid closed until blackened, about 6 minutes. Serve as directed.

Per sandwich: 404 calories, 34 g protein, 6 g fat (1 g sat), 66 g carbs, 708 mg sodium, 109 mg calcium, 8 g fiber

Note: Analysis doesn't include burger toppings.

Cook Smart

- If you like, the patties can be frozen after steaming. Mist a baking sheet with cooking spray. Unwrap the burgers and put them on the baking sheet. Freeze until solid. The burgers can then be packaged in a ziplock bag and frozen for up to 3 months.

Harissa paste, a North African condiment, is a flavorful blend of chiles and spices that contributes a unique flavor to these burgers. I like to serve them on toasted English muffins spread with vegan mayonnaise and topped with thinly sliced tomatoes, cucumbers, dill pickles, and a few romaine lettuce leaves to up the freshness factor.

HARISSA SEITAN BURGERS

See photo facing page 45.

Yield: 8 sandwiches

1 teaspoon canola oil

½ cup chopped onion

3 cloves garlic, minced

2 teaspoons ground coriander

1 teaspoon ground cumin

1 teaspoon smoked paprika

1 teaspoon ground turmeric

½ teaspoon ground pepper

8 ounces tempeh

3 tablespoons nutritional yeast flakes

3 tablespoons harissa paste, homemade (page 160) or store-bought

Heat the oil in a small skillet over medium heat. Add the onion and cook, stirring occasionally, until translucent, about 4 minutes. Add the garlic, coriander, cumin, paprika, turmeric, and pepper and cook, stirring constantly, for 1 to 2 minutes to lightly toast the spices.

Put the tempeh in a food processor and process until it forms crumbs. Add the onion mixture, nutritional yeast, harissa paste, lemon juice, tamari, and liquid smoke and process until mixed. Add the vital wheat gluten and broth and process until the mixture pulls away from the work bowl and gluten threads are visible, 2 to 3 minutes.

Tear off eight 12-inch pieces of foil. Divide the mixture into 8 equal portions. Put each portion on a piece of foil and form into a patty about 3½ inches in diameter. Fold the foil around the patties but don't seal it tightly, as the patties will expand during steaming. Steam for 40 minutes. Refrigerate before grilling for optimum texture. The patties may also be frozen after steaming (see Cook Smart, page 67).

Preheat a grill, grill pan, or electric grill to medium-high heat.

Juice from ½ lemon

1 tablespoon reduced-
    sodium tamari

2 teaspoons liquid smoke

¾ cup vital wheat gluten

¼ cup salt-free vegetable broth

Vegan mayonnaise
    (optional), for serving

8 burger buns or English
    muffins, split and
    grilled if desired

Favorite burger toppings,
    such as lettuce, tomato,
    pickles, and onion

Lightly oil the grill with canola oil. Put the patties on the grill. Cook until marked, about 4 minutes. Turn over and cook until the other side is marked, about 4 minutes. (If using an electric grill, keep it open and cook a few minutes longer if necessary.)

Spread vegan mayonnaise on the cut sides of the buns if desired. Put the patties on the bottom halves of the buns. Cover with toppings as desired and the top halves of the buns.

Per sandwich: 244 calories, 21 g protein, 6 g fat (2 g sat), 37 g carbs, 321 mg sodium, 94 mg calcium, 3 g fiber

Note: Analysis doesn't include vegan mayonnaise or burger toppings.

Cook Smart

• Turmeric stains surfaces easily. Shape the burgers right on the foil to avoid extra cleanup.

Grilled cheese sandwiches are a standby, even in many vegan homes. This version, built on homemade bread hot off the grill, is topped with fresh tomatoes and basil for the perfect combination of flavors and textures.

GROWN-UP GRILLED CHEESE

Yield: 2 sandwiches, 4 servings • *Advance prep: The dough must rise for 2 hours.*

Bread

1½ cups all-purpose flour, plus more if needed

1 cup white whole wheat flour (see Cook Smart)

½ teaspoon salt

1 cup warm water (about 105 degrees F)

2¼ teaspoons active dry yeast

1 teaspoon sugar

1 tablespoon extra-virgin olive oil

To make the bread, put both flours and the salt in a medium bowl and stir to combine.

Put the water, yeast, and sugar in a small bowl and stir to combine. Set aside for about 5 minutes to proof; the yeast is ready when the mixture bubbles. Stir in the oil. Pour into the flour mixture and stir well to form a cohesive dough.

Turn the dough out onto a lightly floured work surface and knead until smooth, about 8 minutes. The dough should be slightly sticky but not wet. If necessary, knead in more flour, 1 tablespoon at a time, to achieve the proper consistency. Form the dough into a ball.

Mist a large bowl with olive oil spray. Put the dough in the bowl and turn to coat with the oil. Cover with a clean kitchen towel and let rise in a warm place until doubled in size, about 1½ hours (see Cook Smart, page 39).

Transfer the dough to a lightly floured work surface. Divide into 4 equal pieces and form each into a ball. Cover with the towel and let rest for 30 minutes.

To make the topping, put all the ingredients in a medium bowl and stir gently to combine. Season with salt to taste if desired.

Electric Grill Method

Preheat an electric grill to high heat.

Working on a lightly floured work surface, roll each ball of dough out to an 8- to 10-inch round. Cook the rounds one at a time, closing the grill and cooking until golden and marked, about 3 minutes.

To assemble the sandwiches, sprinkle ¼ cup of the vegan cheese on two of the rounds. Lay a second round on top of each. Cook

Topping

2 large tomatoes, preferably heirloom, seeded and chopped

¼ cup minced fresh basil

2 cloves garlic, minced

1 teaspoon extra-virgin olive oil

Pinch ground pepper

Salt (optional)

Cheese

½ cup shredded vegan mozzarella cheese (see Cook Smart)

the sandwiches one at a time, closing the grill and cooking until the cheese is melted, 3 to 5 minutes. Spread half of the topping over each sandwich. Cut into quarters to serve.

Outdoor Grill or Grill Pan Method

Preheat an outdoor grill or grill pan to medium-high heat.

Roll out the rounds as directed. Put them on the grill or grill pan and cook until marked, 2 to 4 minutes, working in batches if using a grill pan. Turn over and cook until the other side is marked, 2 to 4 minutes.

To assemble the sandwiches, sprinkle ¼ cup of vegan cheese on two of the rounds. Lay a second round on top of each. Cook until the cheese is melted, 3 to 5 minutes. Top and serve the sandwiches as directed.

Per serving: 364 calories, 11 g protein, 9 g fat (2 g sat), 61 g carbs, 431 mg sodium, 33 mg calcium, 7 g fiber

Cook Smart

- Although "white whole wheat flour" may sound like some sort of white flour, it's actually whole wheat flour made from white wheat rather than red wheat.
- If you're a big fan of vegan cheese, add 2 tablespoons more cheese to each sandwich. (However, those who tested this recipe found the amount called for to be just right.)
- This bread can be used in any sandwich. Put whatever ingredients you prefer on one piece of bread, top with a second piece of bread, and return to the grill.

Grilled portobellos are a perennial favorite. If you haven't tried them before, just one bite will reveal why they are so popular. Make extras, as the aroma may have neighbors flocking to your backyard to see what they're missing.

BBQ PORTOBELLO GRILLERS

Yield: 4 sandwiches ● *Advance prep: Make Barbecue Sauce in a Flash (page 165).*

¼ cup dry red wine

1 teaspoon reduced-
   sodium tamari

¼ teaspoon ground pepper

4 portobello mushrooms,
   stems and gills removed

1 cup Barbecue Sauce in
   a Flash (page 165)

4 burger buns, split and
   grilled if desired

Favorite burger toppings,
   such as lettuce, tomatoes,
   pickles, and onion

Put the wine, tamari, and pepper in a small bowl and stir to combine. Mist the tops of the mushrooms with olive oil spray. Put the mushrooms in a 13 x 9-inch nonreactive baking pan stem-side up. Pour the wine mixture evenly over the mushrooms and let marinate at room temperature for 30 minutes.

Preheat a grill, grill pan, or electric grill to medium-high heat.

Lightly oil the grill with canola oil. Put the mushrooms on the grill stem-side up and cook until marked, about 5 minutes, occasionally pressing the mushrooms down with a turner to create more contact with the grill, and basting with about half of the barbecue sauce. Turn over and cook in the same fashion, basting with the remaining barbecue sauce, until the other side is marked and the flesh is soft and tender in the center, about 5 minutes. Cook 2 minutes longer, until the sauce thickens and coats the mushrooms. (If using an electric grill, keep it open and cook a few minutes longer if necessary.)

Put the mushrooms on the bottom halves of the buns. Cover with toppings as desired and the top halves of the buns.

Per sandwich: 266 calories, 10 g protein, 3 g fat (0.4 g sat), 66 g carbs, 932 mg sodium, 44 mg calcium, 3 g fiber

Note: Analysis doesn't include burger toppings.

Chapter 4

Mouthwatering Main Dishes

This spiced noodle salad is filled with crunchy fresh vegetables and topped with savory grilled portobello mushrooms to create an ideal meal.

RAMEN-BROCCOLI SALAD
WITH GRILLED PORTOBELLOS

Yield: 4 servings ● *Advance prep: Make Teriyaki Sauce (page 166).*

Ramen-Broccoli Salad

Noodles from 4 packages
(2 ounces each) ramen,
broken apart

Seasoning packets from
the ramen (optional; see
Cook Smart, page 49)

4 cups shredded broccoli
stalks (see Cook Smart)

Juice from 1 lime

1 tablespoon seasoned
rice vinegar

½ to 1 teaspoon red
pepper flakes

1½ cups Teriyaki Sauce
(page 166)

1 cup slivered red bell pepper

1 cup minced scallions

1 cup trimmed and sliced
snow peas, in 1-inch pieces

Pinch ground pepper

Salt (optional)

To make the salad, bring a large pot of water to a boil over high heat. Add the noodles and optional seasoning packets and decrease the heat to medium-high. Cook, stirring occasionally, until the noodles are tender but still firm, about 3 minutes. Drain and rinse under cold water to stop the cooking. Drain again.

Put the noodles, broccoli stalks, lime juice, vinegar, and ½ teaspoon of the red pepper flakes in a large bowl and toss to combine. Add the teriyaki sauce, bell pepper, scallions, snow peas, and pepper and toss again. Season with salt to taste and more of the red pepper flakes if desired. Cover and refrigerate for at least 30 minutes to allow the flavors to meld.

To prepare the mushrooms, mist them with olive oil spray. Put them in a 13 x 9-inch nonreactive baking pan stem-side up.

Put the broth, tamari, vinegar, five-spice powder, and pepper in a small bowl and stir to combine. Pour the mixture evenly over the mushrooms and let marinate at room temperature for 30 minutes.

Preheat a grill, grill pan, or electric grill to medium-high heat.

Lightly oil the grill with canola oil. Put the mushrooms on the grill stem-side up. Cook until marked, about 5 minutes. Turn over and cook until the other side is marked and the flesh is soft and tender in the center, about 5 minutes. (If using an electric grill, keep it open and cook a few minutes longer if necessary.)

Grilled Portobellos

4 portobello mushrooms, stems and gills removed

2 tablespoons salt-free vegetable broth

1 tablespoon reduced-sodium tamari

1¼ teaspoons seasoned rice vinegar

¼ teaspoon five-spice powder

¼ teaspoon ground pepper

Garnish

Minced scallions

Toasted sesame seeds

To assemble and garnish the dish, divide the salad evenly among four plates. Cut each mushroom into ½-inch-thick slices. Fan the slices from 1 mushroom over each serving. Sprinkle scallions and sesame seeds over the top.

Per serving: 611 calories, 22 g protein, 16 g fat (7 g sat), 103 g carbs, 1,070 mg sodium, 84 mg calcium, 8 g fiber

Note: Analysis doesn't include scallions and toasted sesame seeds for garnish.

Cook Smart

- Broccoli stalks are the sweetest part of broccoli, but they are often discarded. For convenience, you can substitute 12 ounces of store-bought broccoli slaw. Add it to the noodles during the last 15 seconds of cooking just to brighten the color; it should still retain some crunch.

Adzuki beans, sometimes labeled "azuki" beans, are small red beans popular in Japanese cuisine, where they are used most often in desserts. They are also excellent in savory dishes, such as this crunchy salad, which has a delectable dressing with a rich flavor, thanks to the tahini.

ADZUKI BEAN SALAD
WITH SCALLION-TAHINI DRESSING

Yield: 4 servings • *Advance prep: Make Scallion-Tahini Dressing (page 178).*

2 zucchini, quartered
  lengthwise

6 cups chopped
  romaine lettuce

2 (15-ounce) cans adzuki
  beans, drained and rinsed

3 cups chopped
  Chinese cabbage

1 cup chopped snow peas

4 cloves garlic, minced

1 tablespoon grated
  fresh ginger

1 cup Scallion Tahini
  Dressing (page 178),
  plus more if desired

Put the zucchini on the grill cut-side down and cook until marked, about 3 minutes. Turn over and cook until the other cut side is marked, about 3 minutes. (If using an electric grill, keep it open and cook a few minutes longer if necessary.)

When the zucchini are cool enough to handle, cut them crosswise into 1/2-inch pieces. Put the zucchini, lettuce, beans, cabbage, snow peas, garlic, and ginger in a large bowl and toss gently to combine. Drizzle the dressing over the top and toss to coat. Taste and add more dressing if desired.

Per serving: 360 calories, 19 g protein, 4 g fat (1 g sat), 65 g carbs, 292 mg sodium, 168 mg calcium, 19 g fiber

Make this Italian salad in summer, when tomatoes are at their best. This updated version adds even more vegetables, along with tempeh for a protein boost, and nestles the salad on a bed of fresh arugula. When making the Italian Tempeh for this salad, be sure to reserve any leftover marinade for basting the vegetables as they grill.

PANZANELLA WITH TEMPEH   See photo between pages 92 and 93.

Yield: 4 servings • Advance prep: Make Italian Tempeh (page 89) and Italian Dressing (page 175).

7 slices ciabatta, about
   1 inch thick

1 zucchini, cut lengthwise
   into ½-inch-thick slabs
   (see Cook Smart)

1 red bell pepper, cut into
   ½-inch-thick rings

3 slices red onion,
   about ½ inch thick

8 ounces Italian Tempeh
   (page 89), marinade
   reserved, chopped

1½ pounds tomatoes,
   preferably heirloom,
   seeded and chopped

1 cucumber, peeled,
   seeded, and chopped

1 cup fresh basil leaves,
   lightly packed and torn

½ cup chopped kalamata olives

¾ cup Italian Dressing
   (page 175)

4 cups arugula, lightly packed

Preheat a grill, grill pan, or electric grill to medium heat.

Lightly oil the grill with canola oil. Put the bread on the grill and cook until marked, about 4 minutes. Turn over and cook until the other side is marked, about 3 minutes. (If using an electric grill, keep it open for both the bread and the vegetables and cook a few minutes longer if necessary.) Tear the bread into bite-sized pieces.

Put the zucchini, bell pepper, and onion on the grill and cook until marked, about 5 minutes, occasionally basting with the reserved marinade. Turn over and cook in the same fashion until the other side is marked, about 5 minutes.

When the pepper, zucchini, and onion are cool enough to handle, chop them and put them in a large bowl. Add the tempeh, tomatoes, cucumber, basil, olives, and bread and stir gently to combine. Add ½ cup of the dressing and toss to coat.

Divide the arugula evenly among four plates and top with the tempeh mixture. Serve with the remaining dressing on the side.

Per serving: 593 calories, 26 g protein, 22 g fat (4 g sat), 79 g carbs, 641 mg sodium, 111 mg calcium, 8 g fiber

Cook Smart
• After preparing the tempeh, put the zucchini in the leftover marinade prior to grilling for extra flavor.

Lighter salads have their place on the table, but this salad is a meal in itself and substantial enough to satisfy even the heartiest appetites. The fresh vegetables provide a wonderful contrast to the grill flavor of the seitan and potatoes, and the creamy, zesty dressing accents the dish beautifully.

SEITAN AND POTATO SALAD
WITH HORSERADISH DRESSING

Yield: 8 servings

Advance prep: Make Seitan Roasts (page 90) and All-Purpose Dry Rub (page 158). Soak the cashews for 1 hour.

Horseradish Dressing

3 tablespoons cashews, soaked in cold water for 1 hour and drained

3 tablespoons unsweetened soy milk

3 tablespoons cider vinegar

1 shallot, chopped

1 tablespoon vegan prepared horseradish

½ teaspoon light brown sugar

Pinch ground pepper

Salt (optional)

To make the dressing, put the cashews, soy milk, vinegar, shallot, horseradish, brown sugar, and pepper in a small blender and process until smooth. Season with salt to taste if desired. The dressing can be used immediately or may be stored in a covered container in the refrigerator for up to 1 week.

To make the salad, put the potatoes in a medium saucepan and add water to cover. Bring to a boil over medium-high heat. Decrease the heat to low and simmer uncovered until fork-tender, about 8 minutes. Transfer the potatoes to a large bowl with a slotted spoon, reserving the hot water in the saucepan. Drizzle the vinegar over the potatoes and toss gently to coat.

Put the saucepan of water over medium-high heat and bring to a boil. Add the green beans and cook for 2 minutes. Drain and rinse under cold water to stop the cooking. Drain again.

Preheat a grill, grill pan, or electric grill to medium heat.

Rub the All-Purpose Dry Rub evenly over the seitan slices. Lightly oil the grill with canola oil.

Put the potatoes on the grill. Cook until marked, about 3 minutes. Return the potatoes to the bowl. (If using an electric grill, keep it open

Salad

12 ounces red potatoes,
  scrubbed and cut
  into 2-inch cubes

1 tablespoon cider vinegar

1 cup sliced green beans,
  in 1-inch pieces

1 tablespoon All-Purpose
  Dry Rub (page 158)

1 pound Seitan Roasts
  (page 90), cut into
  ½-inch-thick slices

6 cups mixed salad greens

1 cup cherry tomatoes, halved

1 carrot, shredded

2 radishes, sliced

2 slices red onion, about
  ½ inch thick, quartered

for both the potatoes and the seitan, and cook a few minutes longer if necessary.)

Put the seitan slices on the grill and cook until marked, about 4 minutes. Turn over and cook until the other side is marked, about 4 minutes.

Put the green beans, salad greens, tomatoes, carrot, radishes, and onion in the bowl with the potatoes and stir gently to combine. Divide the salad evenly among four plates. Top with the seitan slices and drizzle with the dressing.

Per serving: 229 calories, 20 g protein, 2 g fat (0.3 g sat), 25 g carbs, 862 mg sodium, 121 mg calcium, 5 g fiber

Smoky, a little sweet, and a little crunchy, the enticing blend of ingredients in this recipe results in a gourmet treat. For an eye-catching salad plate, mound the salad evenly on the greens, surround each serving with carrot and celery sticks, and offer crackers on the side. This salad also makes a super sandwich filling.

SMOKY SEITAN SALAD
WITH POMEGRANATE SEEDS

See photo facing page 92.

Yield: 6 servings

Advance prep: Make Classic Cutlets (page 91) and Smoke Booster (page 161). Marinate the cutlets for at least 8 hours.

Smoky Seitan

½ cup Smoke Booster
   (page 161)

1 tablespoon reduced-
   sodium tamari

1 teaspoons hot sauce

2 teaspoons balsamic vinegar

1 teaspoon herbes de Provence

1 teaspoon maple syrup

¼ teaspoon salt

⅛ teaspoon ground pepper

4 Classic Cutlets (page 91)

Salad

½ cup chopped grilled
   onion (see page 14)

½ cup pomegranate seeds

⅓ cup minced celery

¼ cup slivered blanched
   almonds

3 tablespoons vegan
   mayonnaise, plus
   more if desired

1 tablespoon minced fresh
   thyme, or 1 teaspoon dried

¼ teaspoon dried tarragon

3 cups salad greens,
   lightly packed

To prepare the seitan, put the Smoke Booster, tamari, hot sauce, vinegar, herbes de Provence, maple syrup, salt, and pepper in a 13 x 9-inch nonreactive baking pan and stir to combine. Add the cutlets and turn to coat. Cover and refrigerate for 8 hours or up to 3 days, turning the cutlets occasionally.

Preheat a grill, grill pan, or electric grill to medium-high heat.

Lightly oil the grill with canola oil. Put the cutlets on the grill, reserving the marinade. Cook until marked, about 5 minutes, while occasionally basting with the marinade. Turn over and cook in the same fashion until the other side is marked, about 5 minutes longer. (If using an electric grill, keep it open and cook a few minutes longer if necessary.)

When the cutlets are cool enough to handle, dice them and put them in a medium bowl.

To assemble the salad, put the onion, pomegranate seeds, celery, almonds, vegan mayonnaise, thyme, and tarragon in the bowl with the diced cutlets and stir to combine. Add up to 1 tablespoon additional vegan mayonnaise for a moister consistency if desired.

Divide the greens evenly among six plates and top with the cutlet mixture.

Per serving: 305 calories, 18 g protein, 12 g fat (1 g sat), 20 g carbs, 936 mg sodium, 143 mg calcium, 5 g fiber

This versatile dish takes only minutes to prepare once the tofu has marinated. These tofu triangles make an appearance in this book atop Porcini and Sausage Paella (page 118), and they also work well in salads or sandwiches.

TANGY TOFU TRIANGLES

Yield: 4 servings ● *Advance prep: Press the tofu and then marinate it for at least 2 hours.*

⅓ cup salt-free vegetable broth

1 tablespoon minced jalapeño chile

1 tablespoon freshly squeezed lemon juice

1 tablespoon olive oil

1 tablespoon red wine vinegar

2 teaspoons minced shallot

2 cloves garlic, minced

1 teaspoon agave nectar

1 teaspoon smoked paprika

¾ teaspoon salt

½ teaspoon lemon pepper

¼ teaspoon dried thyme

¼ teaspoon ground pepper

1 pound extra-firm tofu, pressed (see page 14), cut into 8 slabs, then cut diagonally into triangles

Put the broth, chile, lemon juice, oil, vinegar, shallot, garlic, agave nectar, paprika, salt, lemon pepper, thyme, and pepper in a small blender and process until smooth. Pour the marinade into a 13 x 9-inch nonreactive baking pan. Add the tofu and turn to coat. Cover and refrigerate for 2 hours or up to 3 days, turning the tofu occasionally.

Preheat a grill, grill pan, or electric grill to medium-high heat.

Lightly oil the grill with canola oil. Put the tofu on the grill, reserving the marinade. Cook until marked, about 5 minutes, while occasionally basting with the marinade. Turn over and cook in the same fashion until the other side is marked, about 5 minutes longer. (If using an electric grill, keep it open and cook a few minutes longer if necessary.)

Per serving: 194 calories, 17 g protein, 12 g fat (2 g sat), 4 g carbs, 277 mg sodium, 135 mg calcium, 0 g fiber

Combining Smoke Booster with coffee and a hint of harissa paste creates layers of flavor in this subtle marinade. I especially like this tofu slathered with Creamy Harissa Sauce (page 172) for a double dose of Middle Eastern flair.

RED-EYE TOFU STEAKS

See photo facing page 93.

Yield: 4 servings • *Advance prep: Make Smoke Booster (page 161). Press the tofu and then marinate it for at least 8 hours.*

½ cup Smoke Booster (page 161)

¼ cup brewed coffee

2 tablespoons seasoned rice vinegar

1 clove garlic, minced

½ teaspoon agave nectar

½ teaspoon harissa paste, homemade (page 160) or store-bought

½ teaspoon prepared yellow mustard

¼ teaspoon salt

Pinch ground pepper

1 pound extra-firm tofu, pressed (see page 14) and cut into 8 slabs

Put the Smoke Booster, coffee, vinegar, garlic, agave nectar, harissa paste, mustard, salt, and pepper in a 13 x 9-inch nonreactive baking pan and stir to combine. Add the tofu and turn to coat. Cover and refrigerate for 8 hours or up to 3 days, turning the tofu occasionally.

Preheat a grill, grill pan, or electric grill to medium-high heat.

Lightly oil the grill with canola oil. Put the tofu on the grill, reserving the marinade. Cook until marked, about 5 minutes, while occasionally basting with the marinade. Turn over and cook in the same fashion until the other side is marked, about 5 minutes. (If using an electric grill, keep it open and cook a few minutes longer if necessary.)

Per serving: 193 calories, 17 g protein, 11 g fat (2 g sat), 6 g carbs, 436 mg sodium, 134 mg calcium, 2 g fiber

Vegan kitchens just can't have enough grilled tofu recipes. This appealing version uses five-spice powder, a Chinese seasoning blend that traditionally consists of star anise, cloves, cinnamon, fennel seeds, and Sichuan pepper. This tasty tofu is wonderful in wraps.

FIVE-SPICE TOFU

Yield: 4 servings • Advance prep: Press the tofu and then marinate it for at least 8 hours.

3 tablespoons reduced-sodium tamari

2 tablespoons freshly squeezed lime juice

2 tablespoons mirin

3 cloves garlic, minced

1 tablespoon sriracha sauce

1½ teaspoons dark brown sugar

¾ teaspoon five-spice powder

1 pound extra-firm tofu, pressed (see page 14) and cut into 4 slabs

Put the tamari, lime juice, mirin, garlic, sriracha sauce, brown sugar, and five-spice powder in a 13 x 9-inch nonreactive baking pan and stir to combine. Add the tofu and turn to coat. Cover and refrigerate for 8 hours or up to 3 days, turning the tofu occasionally.

Preheat a grill, grill pan, or electric grill to medium-high heat.

Lightly oil the grill with canola oil. Put the tofu on the grill, reserving the marinade. Cook until marked, about 5 minutes, while occasionally basting with the marinade. Turn over and cook in the same fashion until the other side is marked, about 5 minutes longer. (If using an electric grill, keep it open and cook a few minutes longer if necessary.)

Per serving: 205 calories, 19 g protein, 11 g fat (2 g sat), 9 g carbs, 643 mg sodium, 135 mg calcium, 0 g fiber

White wine helps pack these tofu slices with umami. With its enticing blend of seasonings, this tofu is a terrific main dish as is, or try it in the Italian Tofu Sandwiches (page 58) or Linguine Puttanesca with Tofu (page 109).

TOFU ITALIANO

Yield: 4 servings ● Advance prep: Press the tofu and then marinate it for at least 1 hour.

3 tablespoons dry white wine

1 tablespoon salt-free
   vegetable broth

1 tablespoon balsamic vinegar

2 teaspoons olive oil

1 teaspoon nutritional
   yeast flakes

½ teaspoon garlic powder

½ teaspoon Italian
   seasoning blend

½ teaspoon onion powder

¼ teaspoon red pepper flakes

Generous pinch
   ground pepper

1 pound extra-firm tofu,
   pressed (see page 14)
   and cut into 8 slabs

Put the wine, broth, vinegar, oil, nutritional yeast, garlic powder, Italian seasoning blend, onion powder, red pepper flakes, and pepper in a 13 x 9-inch nonreactive baking pan and stir to combine. Add the tofu and turn to coat. Cover and refrigerate for 1 hour or up to 3 days, turning the tofu occasionally.

Preheat a grill, grill pan, or electric grill to medium-high heat.

Lightly oil the grill with canola oil. Put the tofu on the grill, reserving the marinade. Cook until marked, about 5 minutes, while occasionally basting with the marinade. Turn over and cook in the same fashion until the other side is marked, about 5 minutes. (If using an electric grill, keep it open and cook a few minutes longer if necessary.)

Per serving: 213 calories, 18 g protein, 13 g fat (2 g sat), 5 g carbs, 219 mg sodium, 135 mg calcium, 0 g fiber

Chimichurri sauce, which originated in Argentina, is best known in its green incarnation made with parsley, but red versions are also traditional and popular. Although red chimichurri sauce complements many grilled foods, including tempeh and portobello mushrooms, I'm partial to using it with tofu, as in this recipe.

GRILLED TOFU
WITH RED-HOT CHIMICHURRI SAUCE

See photo between pages 92 and 93.

Yield: 4 servings

Advance prep: Make Red-Hot Chimichurri Sauce (page 168). Press the tofu and then marinate it for at least 1 hour.

1 tablespoon reduced-sodium tamari

1 pound extra-firm tofu, pressed (see page 14) and cut into 8 slabs

1 cup Red-Hot Chimichurri Sauce (page 168)

2 tablespoons salt-free vegetable broth

Put the tamari in a 13 x 9-inch nonreactive baking pan. Add the tofu and turn each piece to coat. Pour ½ cup of the chimichurri sauce over the tofu and turn to coat again. Cover and refrigerate for 1 hour or up to 24 hours.

Preheat a grill, grill pan, or electric grill to medium-high heat.

Lightly oil the grill with canola oil. Put the tofu on the grill, reserving the marinade. Cook until marked, about 5 minutes, while occasionally basting with the marinade. Turn over and cook in the same fashion until the other side is marked, about 5 minutes longer. (If using an electric grill, keep it open and cook a few minutes longer if necessary.)

Put the remaining ½ cup of chimichurri sauce, any remaining marinade, and the broth in a small saucepan over low heat and stir to combine. Heat, stirring occasionally, until steaming, about 4 minutes. To serve, drizzle the sauce over the tofu.

Per serving: 201 calories, 18 g protein, 12 g fat (2 g sat), 6 g carbs, 534 mg sodium, 139 mg calcium, 0 g fiber

Cook Smart

- If serving the tofu with a cooked grain, such as rice or quinoa, stir 2 tablespoons of chimichurri sauce into the cooking water to subtly flavor the grain.

In this impressive dish, marinated grilled tofu is smothered in an herbed mushroom sauce. It's a stunning centerpiece for a formal meal when entertaining, and a wonderful introduction to tofu for those who have never tried it.

SAVORY GRILLED TOFU
WITH MUSHROOM SAUCE

Yield: 4 servings ● *Advance prep: Press the tofu and then marinate it for at least 1 hour.*

Marinated Tofu

3 tablespoons balsamic vinegar

1½ tablespoons ketchup

1½ teaspoons agave nectar

½ teaspoon onion powder

¼ teaspoon garlic powder

¼ teaspoon salt

¼ teaspoon ground pepper

1 pound extra-firm tofu, pressed
    (see page 14) and cut into 8 slabs

Mushroom Sauce

1 tablespoon olive oil

1 shallot, minced

3 tablespoons minced
    red bell pepper

2 tablespoons minced celery

¾ teaspoon dried thyme

½ teaspoon herbes de Provence

12 ounces cremini
    mushrooms, sliced

2 cloves garlic, minced

1 cup salt-free vegetable broth,
    chilled or at room temperature

1 tablespoon cornstarch

1 tablespoon minced fresh
    parsley, for garnish

To prepare the tofu, put the vinegar, ketchup, agave nectar, onion powder, garlic powder, salt, and pepper in a 13 x 9-inch nonreactive baking pan and stir to combine. Add the tofu and turn to coat. Cover and refrigerate for 1 hour or up to 3 days, turning the tofu occasionally.

Preheat a grill, grill pan, or electric grill to medium-high heat.

Lightly oil the grill with canola oil. Put the tofu on the grill, reserving the marinade for the sauce. Cook until marked, about 5 minutes. Turn over and cook until the other side is marked, about 5 minutes. (If using an electric grill, keep it open and cook a few minutes longer if necessary.)

To make the sauce, heat the oil in a large skillet on an outdoor grill or on the stove over medium heat. Add the shallot, bell pepper, celery, thyme, and herbes de Provence and cook, stirring occasionally, until softened, about 3 minutes. Add the mushrooms and garlic. Cook, stirring occasionally, until the mushrooms are just tender, about 3 minutes.

Put the broth and cornstarch in a small bowl and whisk to form a slurry. Pour the slurry and the reserved marinade into the skillet. Cook, stirring constantly, until thickened, about 3 minutes. Put the tofu in the skillet and turn to coat. Cook until the tofu is heated through, about 3 minutes. Serve garnished with the parsley.

Per serving: 262 calories, 21 g protein, 14 g fat (3 g sat), 13 g carbs, 129 mg sodium, 201 mg calcium, 1 g fiber

If you're lucky, you may be able to buy smoked tofu at a local market. Fortunately, you can also make it at home using this recipe or, if you don't have a smoker, using the recipe on page 88. If you make this indoors, keep in mind that it's called "smoked" for a reason. Be prepared: Your smoke alarm is likely to go off.

SMOKED TOFU WITH A SMOKER

Yield: 4 servings • Advance prep: Make Smoke Booster (page 161). Press the tofu and then marinate it for at least 1 hour.

2 tablespoons Smoke Booster (page 161)

2 tablespoons salt-free vegetable broth

1 tablespoon dry red wine or additional broth

½ teaspoon maple syrup

⅛ teaspoon salt

Pinch ground pepper

1 pound extra-firm tofu, pressed (see page 14) and cut into 8 slabs

Put the Smoke Booster, broth, wine, maple syrup, salt, and pepper in a 13 x 9-inch nonreactive baking pan and stir to combine. Add the tofu and turn to coat. Cover and refrigerate for 1 hour or up to 3 days, turning the tofu occasionally.

Prepare a stovetop smoker by adding about 2 tablespoons of wood chips to the bottom. Using the smoker according to the manufacturer's directions, put the tofu on the smoking rack and smoke for at least 30 minutes, turning once halfway through the cooking time. Longer smoking will result in a chewier texture.

Smokers may also be used on an outdoor grill. Follow the manufacturer's directions and cook as directed.

Per serving: 181 calories, 17 g protein, 11 g fat (2 g sat), 4 g carbs, 114 mg sodium, 135 mg calcium, 0 g fiber

If you don't have a smoker, you can still enjoy the irresistible flavors characteristic of smoked tofu—especially if you cook the tofu on a grill and use a smoker box or foil smoke packet (see page 11). This tofu is sensational in sandwiches, salads, soups, and other dishes.

SMOKED TOFU WITHOUT A SMOKER

Yield: 4 servings • Advance prep: Press the tofu and then marinate it for at least 8 hours.

3 tablespoons brewed coffee

1 tablespoon liquid smoke

1 tablespoon reduced-
   sodium tamari

1 tablespoon cider vinegar

2 teaspoons light brown sugar

1 teaspoon onion powder

1 teaspoon smoked paprika

1 teaspoon olive oil

½ teaspoon garlic powder

½ teaspoon vegan
   Worcestershire sauce

⅛ teaspoon ground pepper

1 pound extra-firm tofu,
   pressed (see page 14)
   and cut into 8 slabs

Put the coffee, liquid smoke, tamari, vinegar, brown sugar, onion powder, paprika, oil, garlic powder, vegan Worcestershire sauce, and pepper in a 13 x 9-inch nonreactive baking pan and stir to combine. Add the tofu and turn to coat. Cover and refrigerate for 8 hours or up to 24 hours, turning the tofu occasionally.

Outdoor Method

Cover the grates of an outdoor grill with foil. Preheat the grill to medium-low heat.

Lightly mist the foil with cooking spray. Put the tofu on the foil, reserving the marinade. Cook for about 30 minutes, occasionally basting with the marinade. Turn over and cook in the same fashion until the tofu is browned and firm and has a slightly chewy texture, about 20 minutes.

Indoor Method

Preheat the oven to 250 degrees F. Line a baking sheet with parchment paper or mist it with cooking spray.

Put the tofu on the lined baking sheet, reserving the marinade. Bake for 45 minutes, occasionally basting with the marinade. Turn the tofu over and bake in the same fashion until the tofu is browned and firm and has a slightly chewy texture, about 45 minutes.

Per serving: 199 calories, 18 g protein, 12 g fat (2 g sat), 6 g carbs, 208 mg sodium, 138 mg calcium, 0 g fiber

Cook Smart

• Although this method is designed to not use a smoker, if you have a stovetop smoker, try using it to cook the tofu for an especially rich smoked flavor.

Light and savory, this tempeh is essential for Panzanella with Tempeh (page 77) but be sure to reserve the marinade. Also try this tempeh topped with Bell Pepper and Sun-Dried Tomato Sauce (page 171), or crumble any leftovers for a terrific pizza topping.

ITALIAN TEMPEH

Yield: 4 servings • Advance prep: Make Smoke Booster (page 161). Marinate the tempeh for at least 8 hours.

2 (8-ounce) packages tempeh, poached (see page 14)

½ cup salt-free vegetable broth

½ cup dry red wine

2 tablespoons Smoke Booster (page 161), or 1 teaspoon liquid smoke

1 tablespoon reduced-sodium tamari

1 tablespoon olive oil

4 cloves garlic, minced

2 teaspoons Italian seasoning blend

1 teaspoon onion powder

1 teaspoon ground pepper

Cut each piece of tempeh in half crosswise, then cut the pieces in half laterally to make 8 thin patties.

Put the broth, wine, Smoke Booster, tamari, oil, garlic, Italian seasoning blend, onion powder, and pepper in a 13 x 9-inch nonreactive baking pan and stir to combine. Add the tempeh and turn to coat. Cover and refrigerate for 8 hours or up to 3 days, turning the tempeh occasionally.

Preheat a grill, grill pan, or electric grill to medium-high heat.

Remove the tempeh from the marinade and lightly mist it with olive oil spray. Put the tempeh on the grill and cook until marked, about 7 minutes, occasionally basting with the marinade. Turn over and cook in the same fashion until the other side is marked, about 5 minutes. (If using an electric grill, keep it open and cook a few minutes longer if necessary.)

Per serving: 256 calories, 21 g protein, 15 g fat (4 g sat), 12 g carbs, 123 mg sodium, 113 mg calcium, 0 g fiber

These versatile seitan roasts can be sliced into cutlets or chopped in chunks and incorporated into a variety of dishes. The roasts are flavorful on their own but also stand up to an array of seasonings, so don't hold back if you like to experiment. I always keep some of these in the freezer for easy meals.

SEITAN ROASTS

Yield: Four 8-ounce roasts, 8 servings

2½ cups vital wheat gluten, plus more if needed

½ cup soy flour

¼ cup nutritional yeast flakes

3 cloves garlic, minced

1 teaspoon onion powder

½ teaspoon ground pepper

7 cups salt-free vegetable broth (for Slow Cooker Method), or 4 cups (for Oven Method), chilled, plus more if needed

½ cup dry red wine or additional broth

¼ cup no-salt-added tomato paste

2 tablespoons reduced-sodium tamari

2 tablespoons balsamic vinegar

Per serving (slow cooker method): 205 calories, 33 g protein, 1 g fat (0.1 g sat), 13 g carbs, 196 mg sodium, 7 mg calcium, 1 g fiber

Put the vital wheat gluten, soy flour, nutritional yeast, garlic, onion powder, and pepper in a medium bowl and stir to combine.

Put 1 cup of the broth and the wine, tomato paste, tamari, and vinegar in a small bowl and stir to combine. Pour into the flour mixture and stir with a fork. If necessary, add up to 2 tablespoons more vital wheat gluten or broth to make a firm, workable dough. Knead the dough in the bowl until cohesive, about 2 minutes.

Slow Cooker Method

Divide the dough into 4 equal pieces and shape each piece into a roast. Put the roasts in a slow cooker and pour in the remaining 6 cups of broth, adding more broth if needed to cover the roasts. Cook on low heat for 8 hours.

The texture of the seitan improves as it cools, so let cool completely before using. Cut into serving-size portions to store. Wrapped tightly and stored in a covered container or in ziplock bags, the seitan will keep for 4 days in the refrigerator or 3 months in the freezer.

Oven Method

Preheat the oven to 300 degrees F. Lightly oil a 13 x 9-inch glass baking pan.

Transfer the dough to the prepared pan and spread it evenly. The vital wheat gluten makes an elastic dough, so it will be a little challenging to spread it into the corners of the pan; try letting the mixture rest for 5 minutes to make it easier to spread, and repeat if necessary. Pour in 3 cups of the broth. Cover the pan tightly with foil and put the pan on a baking sheet in case of spillage. Bake for 1 hour. Turn off the heat and leave the seitan in the oven for 1 hour longer. The seitan won't be shaped like a roast, but it can be used in the same way. Store as directed.

These cutlets are standard fare at my house. Seitan is versatile and absorbs seasonings well, making it a tasty stand-in for meat. It's also high in protein and, like all plant-based foods, has no cholesterol.

CLASSIC CUTLETS

Yield: Ten 4-ounce cutlets, 10 servings

2 cups vital wheat gluten,
   plus more if needed

½ cup nutritional yeast flakes

¼ cup chickpea flour

¼ cup soy flour

1 teaspoon garlic powder

1 teaspoon onion powder

¼ teaspoon ground
   white pepper

3¼ cups salt-free vegetable
   broth, plus more if needed

1 tablespoon Dijon mustard

¼ cup dry white wine or
   additional broth

1 teaspoon Italian
   seasoning blend

Preheat the oven to 300 degrees F.

Put the vital wheat gluten, ¼ cup of the nutritional yeast, and the chickpea flour, soy flour, garlic powder, onion powder, and white pepper in a medium bowl and stir to combine. Add 1¼ cups of the broth and the mustard and stir with a fork. If necessary, add up to 2 tablespoons more vital wheat gluten or broth to make a firm, workable dough. Knead the dough in the bowl until cohesive, about 2 minutes. Divide the dough into 10 equal pieces and shape each piece into a ball.

Put the remaining 2 cups of broth, remaining ¼ cup nutritional yeast, and the wine and Italian seasoning blend in a large roasting pan and stir to combine.

Tear off two 10-inch pieces of parchment paper. Sandwich a ball of dough between the pieces of parchment paper. Roll out with a rolling pin to form a cutlet no more than ¼ inch thick. Put the cutlet into the roasting pan and repeat until all of the cutlets are rolled. It's okay if they overlap in the pan a bit.

Cover the pan tightly with foil and bake for 1 hour. Turn off the heat and leave the cutlets in the oven for 1 hour longer.

The texture of the seitan improves as it cools, so let it cool completely before using it. Wrapped tightly and stored in a covered container or in ziplock bags, the cutlets will keep for 4 days in the refrigerator or 3 months in the freezer.

Per serving: 175 calories, 21 g protein, 1 g fat (0.1 g sat), 10 g carbs, 45 mg sodium, 52 mg calcium, 2 g fiber

Once these flavorful cutlets are marinated, they can be on the dinner table within about fifteen minutes. Even though the cutlets are featured here as a main dish, they are also great in sandwiches.

GREAT GARLIC CUTLETS

Yield: 4 servings ● *Advance prep: Make Classic Cutlets (page 91). Marinate the cutlets for at least 1 hour.*

2 tablespoons minced fresh basil, plus more for garnish

2 tablespoons balsamic vinegar

2 tablespoons red wine vinegar

3 cloves garlic, minced

2 teaspoons reduced-sodium tamari

1 teaspoon onion powder

1 teaspoon ketchup

¼ teaspoon ground pepper

4 Classic Cutlets (page 91)

Put the basil, vinegars, garlic, tamari, onion powder, ketchup, and pepper in a 13 x 9-inch nonreactive baking pan and stir to combine. Add the cutlets and turn to coat. Cover and refrigerate for 1 hour or up to 3 days, turning the cutlets occasionally.

Preheat a grill, grill pan, or electric grill to medium-high heat.

Lightly oil the grill with canola oil. Put the cutlets on the grill, reserving the marinade. Cook until marked, about 5 minutes, basting occasionally with the marinade. Turn over and cook in the same fashion until the other side is marked, about 5 minutes. (If using an electric grill, keep it open and cook a few minutes longer if necessary.)

Serve garnished with basil.

Per serving: 183 calories, 21 g protein, 1 g fat (0.1 g sat), 12 g carbs, 116 mg sodium, 56 mg calcium, 2 g fiber

Smoky Seitan Salad with Pomegranate Seeds, p. 80

Panzanella with Tempeh, p. 77

Grilled Tofu with Red-Hot Chimichurri Sauce over quinoa, p. 85

Red-Eye Tofu Steaks, p. 82

Despite the name "five-spice powder," this Chinese seasoning blend often includes more than five ingredients. With that in mind, I've added ginger and coriander to the marinade for these savory cutlets, which are used in Lettuce Wraps (page 44). They can also turn a bowl of Asian Street Soup (page 49) into a meal and are wonderful on salads and in sandwiches and wraps.

ASIAN SPICED CUTLETS

Yield: 4 servings • Advance prep: Make Classic Cutlets (page 91). Marinate the cutlets for at least 1 hour.

4 Classic Cutlets (page 91)

1 tablespoon canola oil

2 cloves garlic, minced

1 teaspoon five-spice powder

1 teaspoon grated fresh ginger

1 teaspoon hot chile oil or
   toasted sesame oil

½ teaspoon ground coriander

½ teaspoon salt

¼ teaspoon ground pepper

Put the cutlets in a 13 x 9-inch nonreactive baking pan. Put the canola oil, garlic, five-spice powder, ginger, oil, coriander, salt, and pepper in a small bowl and stir to combine. Press the mixture onto the cutlets, coating them evenly. Cover and refrigerate for 1 hour or up to 2 days.

Preheat a grill, grill pan, or electric grill to medium-high heat.

Lightly oil the grill with canola oil. Put the cutlets on the grill and cook until marked, about 5 minutes. Turn over and cook until the other side is marked, about 5 minutes. (If using an electric grill, keep it open and cook a few minutes longer if necessary.)

Per serving: 184 calories, 21 g protein, 6 g fat (1 g sat), 10 g carbs, 604 mg sodium, 53 mg calcium, 2 g fiber

When I make Seitan Ribz, I make a lot. That way I can keep plenty of them in the freezer for use in other recipes, such as Seitan and Cucumber Minis (page 43), Teppanyaki Seitan Wraps (page 54), and Coffee-Crusted Ribz (page 96).

SEITAN RIBZ

Yield: 3 pounds, 12 servings ● Advance prep: Make Barbecue Rub (page 158) and Barbecue Sauce in a Flash (page 165).

8 ounces extra-firm tofu, drained

1 cup tomato juice

¾ cup chopped cremini mushrooms

½ cup chopped onion

¼ cup reduced-sodium tamari

2 tablespoons no-salt-added tomato paste

1 tablespoon Barbecue Rub (page 158)

1 tablespoon liquid smoke

2 cloves garlic, minced

2 teaspoons smoked paprika

3¼ cups vital wheat gluten

¼ cup chickpea flour

Preheat the oven to 300 degrees F. Lightly mist a 13 x 9-inch glass baking pan with cooking spray.

Put the tofu, tomato juice, mushrooms, onion, tamari, tomato paste, rub, liquid smoke, garlic, and paprika in a food processor and process until smooth. Add the vital wheat gluten and chickpea flour and process until the mixture pulls away from the work bowl and gluten threads are visible, 2 to 3 minutes.

Transfer the mixture to the prepared pan and spread it evenly. The vital wheat gluten makes an elastic dough, so it will be a little challenging to spread it into the corners of the pan; try letting the mixture rest for 5 minutes to make it easier to spread, and repeat if necessary. Cut the dough in half lengthwise, then cut crosswise nine times to make 20 ribz.

Put the broth, wine, ketchup, vinegar, and pepper in a medium bowl and stir to combine. Pour the mixture evenly over the ribz. Cover the pan tightly with foil and put the pan on a baking sheet in case of spillage. Bake for 1 hour and 15 minutes. Remove the foil, turn off the heat, and leave the ribz in the oven for 1 hour longer. The ribz will flatten out a bit.

The texture of the ribz will improve as they cool, so let them cool completely before using. Wrapped tightly and stored in a covered container or in ziplock bags, the ribz will keep for 1 week in the refrigerator or 3 months in the freezer. Don't grill the ribz until you plan to serve them.

1 cup salt-free vegetable broth

1 cup dry red wine

½ cup ketchup

2 tablespoons cider vinegar

½ teaspoon ground pepper

2 cups Barbecue Sauce in a Flash (page 165; optional), heated until steaming

Preheat a grill, grill pan, or electric grill to medium-high heat.

Lightly oil the grill with canola oil. Put the ribz on the grill and cook until marked, about 6 minutes. Turn over and cook until the other side is marked, about 5 minutes. (If using an electric grill, keep it open and cook a few minutes longer if necessary.)

Serve the ribz with the sauce alongside, if desired.

Per serving: 218 calories, 31 g protein, 3 g fat (0.4 g sat), 15 g carbs, 389 mg sodium, 74 mg calcium, 1 g fiber

Note: Analysis doesn't include Barbecue Sauce in a Flash.

Memphis is famous for its dry-rub ribs, and they were the model for this vegan version. If you're not a purist, try the variation; it includes a "mop," which is a fancy term for "basting sauce." I like the best of all worlds: dry-rub ribz made with a mop and served with Barbecue Sauce in a Flash (page 165) on the side for dipping. The espresso powder brings an intriguing flavor that will keep diners guessing about exactly what is in this dish.

COFFEE-CRUSTED RIBZ

Yield: 6 servings ● *Advance prep: Make Seitan Ribz (page 94). Marinate the ribz for at least 1 hour.*

1½ pounds Seitan
   Ribz (page 94)

¼ cup light brown sugar,
   firmly packed

2 tablespoons instant
   espresso powder

1 teaspoon ground coriander

1 teaspoon smoked paprika

¼ teaspoon ground cayenne

¼ teaspoon ground pepper

Put the ribz in a 13 x 9-inch nonreactive baking pan. Put the brown sugar, espresso powder, coriander, paprika, cayenne, and pepper in a small bowl and stir to combine. Rub the mixture onto the ribz, coating them evenly. Cover and refrigerate for 1 hour or up to 24 hours.

Preheat a grill, grill pan, or electric grill to medium heat.

Lightly oil the grill with canola oil. Put the ribz on the grill and cook until marked, about 6 minutes. Turn over and cook until the other side is marked, about 5 minutes. (If using an electric grill, keep it open and cook a few minutes longer if necessary.)

Per serving: 236 calories, 31 g protein, 3 g fat (0.4 g sat), 20 g carbs, 389 mg sodium, 76 mg calcium, 1 g fiber

SAUCY-RUB RIBZ: For dry-rub ribz that are slightly moist, increase the ingredients to 6 tablespoons of brown sugar, 3 tablespoons of espresso powder, 1½ teaspoons of coriander, 1½ teaspoons of paprika, ⅜ teaspoon of cayenne, and ⅜ teaspoon of pepper. Put ¼ cup of the mixture in a small bowl. Add 2 tablespoons of ketchup and 2 tablespoons of water and stir well to make a thick sauce. Rub the remaining dry mixture over the ribz. When grilling, baste occasionally with the sauce.

The seasonings used for the mushrooms in this recipe are the ideal complement to the Grilled Ratatouille topping the dish. For an even heartier entrée, pile each serving on a slice of grilled garlic bread.

PORTOBELLOS SMOTHERED IN RATATOUILLE

Yield: 4 servings • Advance prep: Make Grilled Ratatouille (page 132).

¼ cup dry red wine

1 teaspoon herbes de Provence

¼ teaspoon salt

⅛ teaspoon ground pepper

4 portobello mushrooms, stems and gills removed

4 cups Grilled Ratatouille (page 132), hot, warm, or at room temperature

Put the wine, herbes de Provence, salt, and pepper in a small bowl and stir to combine. Lightly mist the mushrooms with olive oil spray. Put the mushrooms in a 13 x 9-inch nonreactive baking pan stem-side up. Pour the wine mixture evenly over the mushrooms and let marinate at room temperature for 30 minutes.

Preheat a grill, grill pan, or electric grill to medium-high heat.

Lightly oil the grill with canola oil. Put the mushrooms on the grill, reserving the marinade. If using an outdoor grill, close the lid. Cook until marked, about 5 minutes, occasionally basting with the marinade. Turn over and cook in the same fashion until the other side is marked and the flesh is soft and tender in the center, about 5 minutes. (If using an electric grill, keep it open and cook a few minutes longer if necessary.)

Serve the mushrooms topped with the ratatouille.

Per serving: 176 calories, 6 g protein, 6 g fat (1 g sat), 23 g carbs, 125 mg sodium, 47 mg calcium, 10 g fiber

Piquant Habanero Marinade imparts wonderful Latin American flair to the seitan in these fajitas. Crisp grilled vegetables add to the texture, and lush, creamy avocados add richness and temper the spice.

SEITAN AND AVOCADO FAJITAS

Yield: 6 servings

Advance prep: Make Seitan Roasts (page 163) and Habanero Marinade (page 90). Marinate the seitan for at least 1 hour.

½ cup Habanero Marinade (page 163)

1 teaspoon dried oregano

½ teaspoon dried thyme

12 ounces Seitan Roasts (page 90), cut into ½-inch-thick slices

1 red onion, cut into ½-inch-thick rounds

1 green bell pepper, cut into ½-inch-thick rings

2 avocados, sliced

6 (10-inch) flour tortillas, warmed (see Cook Smart, page 52)

Favorite toppings, such as shredded lettuce, chopped tomatoes, vegan sour cream, or salsa

Put the marinade, oregano, and thyme in an 11 x 7-inch nonreactive baking pan and stir to combine. Add the seitan and turn to coat. Cover and refrigerate for 1 hour or up to 3 days, turning the seitan occasionally.

Preheat a grill, grill pan, or electric grill to medium heat.

Lightly spray the grill with cooking spray. Put the onion, bell pepper, and seitan on the grill, reserving the marinade. Cook until marked, about 5 minutes for the onion and bell pepper and about 6 minutes for the seitan, occasionally basting the seitan with the marinade. (If using an electric grill, keep it open and cook a few minutes longer if necessary.)

When the grilled ingredients are cool enough to handle, cut the onion slices in half and separate the layers. Cut the pepper rings in half. Cut the seitan into ½-inch-wide strips

Divide the seitan, onion, bell pepper, and avocados evenly among the tortillas. Add other toppings as desired. Fold in half and serve.

Per serving: 324 calories, 22 g protein, 11 g fat (2 g sat), 40 g carbs, 489 mg sodium, 92 mg calcium, 6 g fiber

Note: Analysis doesn't include fajita toppings.

Meat and potatoes, move over! Here's a vegan version, assembled on a skewer and bathed in barbecue sauce, that's so much more satisfying. Hearty and full of flavor, this recipe is a nod to the traditional American fare that many of us grew up on, updated and greatly improved.

SEITAN-POTATO STICKS

Yield: 6 servings

Advance prep: Make Seitan Roasts (page 90), Barbecue Rub (page 158), and Barbecue Sauce in a Flash (page 165).

12 small red potatoes, scrubbed and cut into bite-sized pieces (see Cook Smart)

1 pound Seitan Roasts (page 90), cut into bite-sized pieces

2 tablespoons Barbecue Rub (page 158)

2 cups Barbecue Sauce in a Flash (page 165), heated until steaming

Soak eight wooden skewers in water for 30 minutes. Alternatively, lightly mist eight metal skewers with cooking spray.

Put the potatoes in a large saucepan and add cold water to cover. Bring to a boil over medium-high heat. Decrease the heat to low and simmer uncovered until just fork-tender, about 10 minutes; don't overcook the potatoes, or they'll fall apart on the skewers. Drain, rinse under cold water to stop the cooking, and let cool.

Preheat a grill, grill pan, or electric grill to medium heat.

Put the seitan and rub in a medium bowl and toss to coat. Thread the seitan and potatoes on the skewers, alternating them. Mist with olive oil spray.

Put the skewers on the grill and, if using an outdoor grill, close the lid. Cook until marked, about 5 minutes. Turn over and cook until the other side is marked, about 5 minutes, basting with the barbecue sauce during the last 2 minutes of cooking. (If using an electric grill, keep it open and cook a few minutes longer if necessary.)

Serve with the remaining sauce on the side.

Per serving: 537 calories, 33 g protein, 1 g fat (0.1 g sat), 108 g carbs, 349 mg sodium, 56 mg calcium, 5 g fiber

Cook Smart

• For the very best marks (and therefore best flavor), cut the potatoes and seitan to the same size. Since they're threaded onto skewers together, this is important, as it will ensure they have equal contact with the grill.

We vegans love our quinoa, and with good reason: it's a nutritional powerhouse, packed with protein, including all of the essential amino acids. Because quinoa originated in the Andes, I couldn't resist seasoning it with Latin American ingredients for the filling in this dish. Poblano chiles vary in heat level. If the ones you get are too spicy, don't worry—the avocado sauce will help cool things down.

QUINOA-STUFFED POBLANOS

Yield: 4 servings ● Advance prep: Make Avocado Sauce (page 173).

Quinoa Filling

½ cup water

¼ cup red quinoa, rinsed

1½ teaspoons no-salt-added tomato paste

½ teaspoon salt

2 teaspoons canola oil

4 ounces vegan chorizo, crumbled

2 tablespoons minced red onion

1 clove garlic, minced

½ teaspoon ground cumin

¼ teaspoon ground pepper

Chiles and Topping

4 poblano chiles

½ cup Avocado Sauce (page 173)

1 cup chopped tomato

Soak eight wooden toothpicks in water for 30 minutes.

To make the filling, put the water, quinoa, tomato paste, and salt in a small saucepan and stir until the tomato paste is dissolved. Bring to a boil over medium-high heat. Decrease the heat to low and cook uncovered until the quinoa is tender and all of the liquid is absorbed, about 20 minutes.

Outdoor Method

Preheat an outdoor grill to medium heat and put a large cast-iron skillet on the grill.

Put the oil in the skillet. Add the chorizo and cook, stirring occasionally, until browned, about 4 minutes. Add the onion, garlic, cumin, and pepper and cook, stirring occasionally, until fragrant, 2 to 3 minutes. Stir in the quinoa and remove from the heat.

To prepare the chiles and assemble the dish, increase the heat to high. Put the chiles on the grill and cook for about 2 minutes. Turn over and cook the other side just until the chiles are tender, about 2 minutes.

When the chiles are cool enough to handle, slice them open lengthwise along one side, leaving the stem end intact. Carefully scoop out the seeds. Fill the chiles with the quinoa mixture. Close the chiles and secure each one crosswise with two of the toothpicks.

Decrease the heat to medium.

Lightly oil the grill with canola oil. Put the chiles on the grill seam-side up and cook until just beginning to blacken, about 3 minutes.

To serve, remove the toothpicks and top with the avocado sauce and tomato.

Indoor Method

Heat the oil in a large skillet on the stove over medium heat and cook the chorizo, onion, garlic, cumin, and pepper as directed. Stir in the quinoa and remove from the heat.

To prepare the chiles and assemble the dish, put a rack near the top of the oven and preheat the broiler.

Put the chiles on a baking sheet and broil for 2 minutes. Turn and broil just until tender, about 2 minutes longer. Remove the chiles from the oven. Turn the oven temperature down to 425 degrees F.

When the chiles are cool enough to handle, seed and fill them as directed. Put the chiles on the baking sheet seam-side up. Bake for about 3 minutes, just until beginning to blacken. Serve as directed.

Per serving: 149 calories, 4 g protein, 7 g fat (1 g sat), 19 g carbs, 590 mg sodium, 39 mg calcium, 5 g fiber

A frittata is an Italian dish that resembles a Spanish omelet. This frittata is packed with protein from the tofu and vegan sausage. Although dried herbs can be used in a pinch, the fresh herbs, along with the arugula, add liveliness, and the spices contribute a depth of flavor. Serve this frittata with a crisp green salad or a platter of sliced fresh tomatoes to round out the meal.

FRESH HERB FRITTATA

Yield: One 8-inch frittata, 6 servings

8 ounces firm silken tofu

3 tablespoons nutritional yeast flakes

Juice from ½ lemon

1 tablespoon reduced-sodium tamari

½ teaspoon salt

4 teaspoons olive oil

½ cup chopped green bell pepper

½ cup minced onion

4 ounces vegan sausage, seitan, or tempeh bacon, chopped

1 cup arugula, lightly packed and chopped

2 cloves garlic, minced

1 pound extra-firm tofu, patted dry and crumbled

Put the silken tofu, nutritional yeast, lemon juice, tamari, and salt in a blender and process until smooth.

Outdoor Method

Preheat an outdoor grill to medium heat and put a large cast-iron skillet on the grill.

Put 3 teaspoons of the oil in the skillet. Add the bell pepper, onion, and vegan sausage and cook, stirring occasionally, until the vegetables are soft, about 3 minutes. Add the arugula and garlic and cook, stirring occasionally, until fragrant, about 2 minutes. Add the crumbled tofu, cumin, paprika, turmeric, red pepper flakes, and white pepper and cook, stirring occasionally, for 3 to 4 minutes. Add the parsley, thyme, and rosemary and stir to combine. Pour in the silken tofu mixture and stir to combine. Remove from the heat.

Oil an 8-inch cast-iron skillet with the remaining teaspoon of oil. Pack the mixture into the smaller skillet, pressing it in firmly and evenly. Put the skillet on the grill and close the lid. Cook until the top of the frittata is golden and the sides pull away from the skillet when gently pried with a knife, 25 to 30 minutes.

Let cool for at least 10 minutes. Cut into wedges and serve hot or at room temperature.

1 teaspoon ground cumin

½ teaspoon smoked paprika

½ teaspoon ground turmeric

¼ teaspoon red pepper flakes

¼ teaspoon ground
white pepper

2 tablespoons minced fresh
parsley, or 2 teaspoons dried

1 tablespoon minced fresh
thyme, or ¼ teaspoon dried

1 teaspoon minced fresh
rosemary, or
¼ teaspoon dried

Indoor Method

Preheat the oven to 350 degrees F. Cook the sausage and tofu mixture in a large skillet on the stove as directed. Pack the mixture into a small skillet and bake until the top of the frittata is golden and the sides pull away from the skillet when gently pried with a knife, 25 to 30 minutes.

Per serving: 225 calories, 20 g protein, 13 g fat (2 g sat), 9 g carbs, 480 mg sodium, 123 mg calcium, 3 g fiber

Bright red sauce tops skewers threaded with marinated seitan cutlets and vegetables, all on a bed of Israeli couscous, a type of semolina pasta, creating a feast for the eyes as well as the taste buds. Unlike tiny yellow North African couscous, which is granulated, Israeli couscous, also known as pearl couscous, is about the size of peppercorns and has a distinctive, nutty flavor.

TUNISIAN SKEWERS
WITH LEMON-KISSED COUSCOUS

Yield: 4 servings ● *Advance prep: Make Classic Cutlets (page 91) and Creamy Harissa Sauce (page 172). Marinate the cutlets for at least 1 hour.*

Tunisian Seitan

½ cup dry white wine

Juice from ½ lemon
(see Cook Smart)

2 cloves garlic, minced

½ teaspoon ground coriander

½ teaspoon ground cumin

½ teaspoon dried thyme

½ teaspoon agave nectar

¼ teaspoon ground
white pepper

12 ounces Classic Cutlets
(page 91), cut into
16 equal-sized pieces
(see Cook Smart)

Lemon-Kissed Couscous

2½ cups water

Grated zest from 1 lemon

½ teaspoon dried thyme

¼ teaspoon ground pepper

2 cups Israeli couscous

To prepare the seitan, put the wine, lemon juice, garlic, coriander, cumin, thyme, agave nectar, and white pepper in an 11 x 7-inch nonreactive baking pan and stir to combine. Add the cutlet pieces and stir to coat. Cover and refrigerate for 1 hour or up to 3 days, stirring occasionally.

About 30 minutes before you start grilling, soak four wooden skewers in water. Alternatively, lightly mist four metal skewers with cooking spray.

To make the couscous, put the water, zest, thyme, and pepper in a medium saucepan. Bring to a boil over medium-high heat. Stir in the couscous. Decrease the heat to low, cover, and cook until the couscous is tender and all of the liquid is absorbed, about 10 minutes. If excess liquid remains, uncover and cook over low heat a few minutes longer.

To assemble, grill, and serve the skewers, remove the cutlet pieces from the marinade, reserving the marinade. Thread the skewers, alternating the cutlet pieces, bell pepper, mushrooms, and onion.

Preheat a grill, grill pan, or electric grill to medium heat.

Outdoor Grill or Grill Pan Method

Lightly oil the grill with canola oil. Put the skewers on the grill and, if using an outdoor grill, close the lid. (There's no need to cover a grill pan.) Cook until marked, about 5 minutes, occasionally basting with

Vegetables

1 red or green bell pepper, cut into 16 equal-sized pieces

8 cremini mushrooms, halved

½ red onion, cut into 8 pieces, then separated into 16 pieces, each with 2 or 3 layers

Toppings

½ cup Creamy Harissa Sauce (page 172), heated until steaming

Minced fresh parsley, for garnish

the marinade. Turn over and cook in the same fashion until the other side is marked, about 5 minutes.

To serve, divide the couscous among four plates and top with the skewers. Drizzle with the harissa sauce and garnish with parsley.

Electric Grill Method

Lightly oil the grill with canola oil. Put the skewers on the grill, close the lid, and cook the skewers without turning for about 8 minutes, until marked. Serve as directed.

Per serving: 568 calories, 30 g protein, 7 g fat (1 g sat), 87 g carbs, 656 mg sodium, 89 mg calcium, 8 g fiber

Cook Smart

- The couscous calls for the zest from 1 lemon. It's easier to zest citrus fruits before juicing them, so grate the zest for the couscous first and then squeeze the juice.
- Cut the cutlets first, then use the pieces as a guide for cutting the vegetables. Having the ingredients roughly the same size ensures that they'll grill evenly once threaded on the skewers.

TUNISIAN CUTLETS: For a simpler dish, leave the cutlets whole and omit the vegetables. Grill the cutlets until marked, about 5 minutes, occasionally basting with the marinade. Turn over and cook in the same fashion until the other side is marked, about 5 minutes. Divide the couscous among four plates. Top with the cutlets. Drizzle with the Creamy Harissa Sauce and garnish with parsley.

This rustic pasta is best made on an outdoor grill. The sauce, which requires only minimal chopping, is chunky and fresh and suffused with smoky undertones.

COWBOY SPAGHETTI

Yield: 8 servings

1 pound spaghetti

2 tablespoons olive oil

10 Roma tomatoes, cut into quarters and seeded

8 ounces cremini mushrooms, halved, or quartered if large

1 (15-ounce) can low-sodium crushed fire-roasted tomatoes

1 (15-ounce) can low-sodium diced fire-roasted tomatoes

½ cup dry red wine or salt-free vegetable broth

4 cloves garlic, sliced

4 teaspoons Italian seasoning blend

½ teaspoon red pepper flakes (see Cook Smart)

¼ teaspoon ground pepper

Bring a large pot of water to a boil over high heat. Add the spaghetti, decrease the heat to medium-high, and cook, stirring occasionally, until tender but still firm, about 10 minutes. Drain and rinse under cold water. Return the spaghetti to the pot, drizzle with 1 tablespoon of the oil, and toss until evenly coated to minimize sticking.

Outdoor Method

Preheat an outdoor grill to medium heat.

Put the Roma tomatoes, mushrooms, crushed tomatoes, diced tomatoes, wine, garlic, Italian seasoning blend, red pepper flakes, pepper, and remaining tablespoon of oil in a 15 x 11-inch foil roasting pan and stir to combine. Put the pan on the grill and cook, stirring occasionally, for 15 minutes.

Meanwhile, mist the bell pepper and onion with olive oil spray. Put them on the grill and cook until marked, about 5 minutes.

When the bell pepper and onion are cool enough to handle, chop them coarsely and add them to the tomato mixture. Add the basil and stir to combine.

Put the vegan sausages on the grill and cook, turning occasionally, until marked, 6 to 8 minutes. When the sausage is cool enough to handle, cut it into 1-inch-thick rounds.

Put the spaghetti in the roasting pan and stir to coat. If the spaghetti isn't warm, cook, tossing occasionally, until steaming. Serve topped with the vegan sausage.

1 bell pepper, any color, cut into ½-inch-thick rings

½ onion, cut into ½-inch-thick rounds

½ cup fresh basil leaves, lightly packed and torn

4 vegan Italian sausages

Indoor Method

Preheat the oven to 400 degrees F. Put the tomato mixture in a 6-quart nonreactive casserole dish. Cover and bake for 20 minutes.

Preheat a grill pan or electric grill to medium heat. Cook the bell pepper and onion as directed. (If using an electric grill, keep it open for the vegetables and vegan sausage and cook a few minutes longer if necessary.) Add the bell pepper, onion, and basil to the tomato mixture and stir to combine. Cook the vegan sausages as directed. Add the spaghetti to the hot sauce and toss. Serve topped with the vegan sausage.

Per serving: 476 calories, 24 g protein, 11 g fat (1 g sat), 65 g carbs, 342 mg sodium, 86 mg calcium, 8 g fiber

Cook Smart

- This recipe is very flexible. Grill your favorite vegetables, such as eggplant, zucchini, or summer squash. Then chop them and stir them in with the basil.
- If you love spicy food, double the amount of red pepper flakes.

Bright green pesto is the perfect sauce for capellini, a pasta slightly thicker than angel hair, and the sweet and juicy Roma tomatoes burst with flavor. Make this at the peak of summer when basil is growing prolifically and tomatoes are at the peak of their season. The Pesto-Topped Tomatoes used in this dish require just four teaspoons of pesto. Because the amount is so small, I recommend that you make the pesto for this recipe first and use a bit of it when preparing the tomatoes.

PESTO PASTA WITH TOMATOES

Yield: 4 servings ● *Advance prep: Make Pesto-Topped Tomatoes (page 34).*

Pine Nut Pesto

¼ cup pine nuts

2 tablespoons nutritional yeast flakes

3 cloves garlic, minced

4 cups fresh basil leaves, lightly packed

¼ cup salt-free vegetable broth

2 tablespoons freshly squeezed lemon juice

2 tablespoons extra-virgin olive oil

¼ teaspoon ground pepper

Salt (optional)

Pasta and Tomatoes

12 ounces capellini or other thin pasta

1 recipe Pesto-Topped Tomatoes (page 34)

To make the pesto, put the pine nuts, nutritional yeast, and garlic in a food processor and process until the pine nuts are finely ground. Add the basil, broth, lemon juice, oil, and pepper and process until smooth. Season with salt to taste if desired. The pesto can be used immediately or may be stored in a covered container in the freezer for up to 3 months.

To cook the pasta and assemble the dish, bring a large pot of water to a boil over high heat. Add the capellini and decrease the heat to medium-high. Cook, stirring occasionally, until tender but still firm, 3 to 4 minutes. Drain and return to the pot. Add the pesto and toss to evenly coat the capellini. Divide evenly among four plates. Top with the Pesto-Topped Tomatoes.

Per serving: 545 calories, 14 g protein, 2 g fat (2 g sat), 82 g carbs, 28 mg sodium, 124 mg calcium, 8 g fiber

Puttanesca sauce is studded with olives and capers and enhanced with a hint of heat. In this version, the spiciness is courtesy of a jalapeño chile and red pepper flakes. The addition of tofu provides a protein boost and rounds out the dish.

LINGUINE PUTTANESCA WITH TOFU

Yield: 6 servings • *Advance prep: Make Tofu Italiano (page 84).*

1 pound linguine

6 teaspoons olive oil

1 onion, cut into quarters

1 jalapeño chile, minced

4 cloves garlic, sliced

8 cups chopped Roma tomatoes

½ cup halved kalamata olives

2 teaspoons Italian seasoning blend

1 teaspoon capers

1 teaspoon red pepper flakes

⅓ cup fresh basil leaves, lightly packed and minced

2 tablespoons minced fresh parsley

1 pound Tofu Italiano (page 84)

Bring a large pot of water to a boil over high heat. Add the linguine, decrease the heat to medium-high, and cook, stirring occasionally, until tender but still firm, about 9 minutes. Drain and rinse under cold water. Return the linguine to the pot, drizzle with 1½ teaspoons of the oil, and toss until evenly coated to minimize sticking.

Heat a grill, grill pan, or electric grill to medium heat.

Brush the cut sides of the onion with 1½ teaspoons of the oil. Put the onion on the grill and cook until marked, about 5 minutes. Turn over and cook until the other cut side is marked, about 4 minutes.

When the onion is cool enough to handle, chop it.

Outdoor Method

Put the remaining 3 teaspoons of oil in a 15 x 11-inch foil roasting pan. Put the pan on the grill and stir in the chile and garlic. Cook until sizzling, 1 to 2 minutes. Add the onion, tomatoes, olives, Italian seasoning blend, capers, and red pepper flakes. Close the grill and cook, stirring occasionally, until the tomatoes have broken down, about 20 minutes. Stir in the basil and parsley.

Add the pasta and toss to coat. If the linguine isn't warm, cook, tossing occasionally, until steaming. Serve topped with the tofu.

Indoor Method

Prepare the sauce in a large skillet over medium heat as directed. Pour the sauce into the pot with the linguine and toss to coat. Heat and serve as directed.

Per serving: 587 calories, 24 g protein, 24 g fat (4 g sat), 70 g carbs, 631 mg sodium, 116 mg calcium, 8 g fiber

Pizza on the grill is a wonderful thing—and probably the closest most of us will come to making wood-fired pizza in our homes. This crispy crust, topped with creamy ranch dressing and tempeh seasoned similarly to Buffalo wings, is proof that pizza can taste decadent even without cheese.

BUFFALO PIZZA

Yield: One 10-inch pizza, 6 servings
Advance prep: The dough must rise for 1½ hours. Make Cashew Ranch Sauce (page 174).

Dough

1½ cups all-purpose flour

½ cup warm water (about 105 degrees F), plus more if needed

1 teaspoon sugar

1 teaspoon active dry yeast

2 teaspoons olive oil

Toppings

8 ounces tempeh, diced

⅓ cup hot sauce

1 tablespoon reduced-sodium tamari

¼ teaspoon garlic powder

¼ teaspoon onion powder

¾ cup Cashew Ranch Sauce (page 174)

½ cup shredded carrot

½ cup sliced roasted red bell pepper (see page 14), or ¼ cup chopped kalamata olives

To make the dough, put the flour in a medium bowl.

Put the water, sugar, and yeast in a small bowl and stir to combine. Set aside for about 5 minutes to proof; the yeast is ready when the mixture bubbles. Stir in the oil. Pour into the flour mixture and stir well to form a cohesive dough. If necessary, add up to 2 tablespoons more water, 1 tablespoon at a time, until the dough comes together.

Turn the dough out onto a lightly floured work surface and knead until smooth and silky, about 6 minutes. Form the dough into a ball.

Lightly mist a medium bowl with cooking spray. Put the dough in the bowl and turn to coat with the oil. Cover with a clean kitchen towel and let rise in a warm place until doubled in size, about 1½ hours (see Cook Smart, page 39).

To prepare the tempeh for the topping, heat a large nonstick skillet over medium heat. Put the tempeh, hot sauce, tamari, garlic powder, and onion powder in the skillet. Cook, stirring occasionally, until the sauce has thickened and coats the tempeh with little or no liquid remaining in the pan, about 10 minutes.

Outdoor Method

Preheat an outdoor grill to medium heat.

Lightly flour a 16-inch piece of parchment paper. Put the dough on the parchment paper and roll it out to a 12-inch round.

Lightly oil the grill with canola oil. Carefully transfer the dough to the grill by inverting it onto the grill and peeling off the parchment paper. Close the lid and cook until marked, about 3 minutes.

Transfer the crust to a cutting board or baking sheet, marked-side up. Spread half of the ranch sauce evenly over the crust to within

$^{1}/_{2}$ inch of the edge. Spread the tempeh, carrot, and bell pepper evenly over the sauce.

Put the pizza back on the grill. Close the lid and cook until the bottom is golden and marked, about 4 minutes. Cut into wedges and serve with the remaining sauce on the side.

Indoor Method

Preheat the oven to 425 degrees F. Roll the dough as directed and put it directly on the oven rack. Peel off the parchment paper and bake for about 3 minutes. Top the pizza as directed and bake for about 15 minutes, until the bottom is golden. Serve as directed.

Per serving: 292 calories, 15 g protein, 12 g fat (4 g sat), 34 g carbs, 504 mg sodium, 68 mg calcium, 2 g fiber

Broccoli and cheese are a classic combination, and encasing them in a crust only adds to the appeal. These calzones are big and hearty; no one will walk away from the table hungry. For easier preparation, make the Tofu Ricotta Sauce in advance.

BROCCOLI AND CHEEZE CALZONES

Yield: 8 calzones

Advance prep: The tofu ricotta sauce must be refrigerated for 2 hours. The dough must rise for 1½ hours.

Tofu Ricotta Sauce

4 cups water

½ cup distilled white vinegar

½ cup sugar

¼ cup nutritional yeast flakes

2 teaspoons Italian seasoning blend

2 cloves garlic, crushed

1 teaspoon salt

1 teaspoon onion powder

1 pound firm tofu, quartered

Juice from ½ lemon

Dough

3 cups all-purpose flour

½ teaspoon salt

1 cup warm water (about 105 degrees F), plus more if needed

2 teaspoons sugar

2 teaspoons active dry yeast

1 tablespoon olive oil

To make the tofu ricotta sauce, put the water, vinegar, sugar, nutritional yeast, Italian seasoning blend, garlic, salt, and onion powder in a medium saucepan and stir to combine. Bring to a boil over medium-high heat. Decrease the heat to low and simmer uncovered for 10 minutes. Remove from the heat, add the tofu, and let cool to room temperature. Cover and refrigerate for 2 hours.

Drain the tofu, discarding the liquid. Put the tofu and lemon juice in a food processor or blender and process until smooth. The tofu ricotta sauce can be used immediately or may be stored in a covered container in the refrigerator up to 1 week. If it separates slightly, stir well before using.

To make the dough, put the flour and salt in a large bowl and stir to combine.

Put the water, sugar, and yeast in a medium bowl and stir to combine. Set aside for about 5 minutes to proof; the yeast is ready when the mixture bubbles. Stir in the oil. Pour into the flour mixture and stir well to form a cohesive dough. If necessary, add up to ¼ cup more water, 1 tablespoon at a time, until the dough comes together.

Turn the dough out onto a lightly floured work surface and knead until smooth and silky, 5 to 6 minutes. Form the dough into a ball.

Lightly mist a large bowl with cooking spray. Put the dough in the bowl and turn to coat with the oil. Cover with a clean kitchen towel and let rise in a warm place until doubled in size, about 1½ hours (see Cook Smart, page 39).

Divide the dough into 4 equal pieces and form each piece into a ball. Cover with the towel, and let rest for 10 minutes.

Broccoli Filling

3 cups small broccoli florets

1 teaspoon olive oil

¼ cup minced shallots

¼ cup minced moist-packed
sun-dried tomatoes

1 tablespoon minced garlic

½ teaspoon dried oregano

½ teaspoon dried thyme

¼ teaspoon ground pepper

Pinch red pepper flakes

3 tablespoons minced
fresh basil

Cheese, Garnish, and
Accompaniment

¾ cup shredded vegan
mozzarella cheese

1 tablespoon minced fresh basil

2 cups marinara sauce

To prepare the filling, steam the broccoli until just tender, about 4 minutes.

Heat the oil in a large skillet over medium heat. Add the shallots, sun-dried tomatoes, garlic, oregano, thyme, pepper, and red pepper flakes. Cook, stirring frequently, until the shallots and garlic are fragrant and have softened, about 3 minutes. Stir in the broccoli and basil.

To assemble and cook the calzones, lightly flour a work surface. Roll out each piece of dough to a 7-inch round. Spread 2 tablespoons of the tofu ricotta sauce on each round. Put one-quarter of the broccoli filling on one side of each round and top with 3 tablespoons of the vegan cheese. Fold the other side of the rounds over to form half-moons. Pinch and seal the edges. Pierce each calzone with a fork one time to allow the calzone to release steam as it bakes.

Outdoor Method

Put a large cast-iron skillet upside down on an outdoor grill to slightly elevate the calzones. Preheat the grill to medium-high heat.

Lightly oil a pizza stone or baking sheet with canola oil. Put the calzones on the stone and then put the stone on the inverted skillet. Close the lid and cook until the calzones are golden, about 7 minutes. If the calzones brown too quickly on the bottom, decrease the heat (see Cook Smart).

Heat the marinara sauce in a grill-safe medium saucepan on the grill or in a medium saucepan on the stove over medium heat, stirring occasionally, until steaming, 3 to 4 minutes.

Serve the marinara sauce on the side, garnished with the basil.

Continued on next page

BROCCOLI AND CHEEZE CALZONES

Continued from page 113

Grill Pan Method

Preheat a grill pan to medium heat.

Lightly oil the grill pan with canola oil. Working in batches if need be, put the calzones on the grill and invert a large heatproof bowl over the grill to create an oven effect. Cook until golden and marked, about 5 minutes. Turn the calzones over and cook in the same fashion until the other side is golden and marked, about 5 minutes. If all of the calzones won't fit under a bowl on the grill pan at the same time, preheat the oven to 300 degrees F. and keep the finished calzones warm in the oven while the others cook.

Heat the marinara sauce in a medium saucepan over low heat, stirring occasionally, until steaming, 3 to 4 minutes. Serve the calzones and sauce as directed.

Per calzone: 368 calories, 13 g protein, 8 g fat (1 g sat), 62 g carbs, 759 mg sodium, 110 mg calcium, 5 g fiber

Cook Smart

- The tofu ricotta sauce makes 2 cups, which is much more than you will need for this recipe. Leftovers can be used as a pizza sauce or sandwich spread.
- When making yeasted bread recipes on an outdoor grill, it's helpful if the grill has more than two burners. Heat the outer burners to a higher temperature and keep the inner burners on lower heat. The outer burners will generate more heat for baking, and you can cook over the inside burners to reduce the chances of burning. To decrease the heat with a charcoal grill, raise the grate.

Sweet and savory, the apricot sauce in this recipe brings out the best in tofu. This is an elegant meal that doesn't require much hands-on time. I recommend serving the skewers over rice to soak up the luscious sauce.

FRUITED TOFU SKEWERS

Yield: 4 servings

Advance prep: Press the tofu and then marinate it for at least 1 hour. Make Savory Apricot Sauce (page 170).

3 tablespoons dry white wine or salt-free vegetable broth

1 tablespoon reduced-sodium tamari

½ teaspoon liquid smoke

1 pound extra-firm tofu, pressed (see page 14) and cut into 12 large cubes

1 green bell pepper, cut into 12 equal-sized pieces

½ red onion, cut into 6 wedges, then separated into 12 pieces, each with 2 or 3 layers

½ cup Savory Apricot Sauce (page 170)

Put the wine, tamari, and liquid smoke in an 8-inch square nonreactive baking pan and stir to combine. Add the tofu and stir gently to coat. Cover and refrigerate for 1 hour or up to 4 hours.

About 30 minutes before you start grilling, soak four wooden skewers in water. Alternatively, lightly mist four metal skewers with cooking spray.

Preheat a grill, grill pan, or electric grill to medium-high heat.

Thread the tofu, bell pepper, and onion on the skewers, alternating them. Put the skewers on a baking sheet and lightly mist with olive oil spray. Brush only the tofu with half of the apricot sauce.

Put the skewers on the grill. Cook until marked, about 7 minutes. Turn the skewers over and cook until the other side is marked, about 4 minutes. (If using an electric grill, keep it open and cook a few minutes longer if necessary.)

Serve with the remaining apricot sauce spooned over the skewers.

Per serving: 247 calories, 19 g protein, 11 g fat (2 g sat), 17 g carbs, 274 mg sodium, 148 mg calcium, 3 g fiber

Think of this as a savory cobbler, or perhaps a unique twist on the ever-popular potpie. Tempeh and chickpeas take well to the spices, while the biscuits give this stew a homey finish.

TEMPEH-CHICKPEA STEW
WITH HARISSA BISCUITS

Yield: 6 servings

Tempeh-Chickpea Stew

2 tablespoons all-purpose flour

1 teaspoon ground coriander

½ teaspoon ground cumin

½ teaspoon ground ginger

¼ teaspoon ground pepper

8 ounces tempeh, poached
   (see page 14), cut into
   1-inch cubes, and kept hot

1 tablespoon olive oil

1 cup chopped onion

1 cup chopped carrots

¾ cup chopped bell
   pepper, any color

¼ cup chopped celery

1 (15-ounce) can chickpeas,
   drained and rinsed

2 cloves garlic, minced

Outdoor Method

To make the stew, preheat an outdoor grill to medium-high heat and put a large cast-iron skillet on the grill.

Put the flour, coriander, cumin, ginger, and pepper in a medium bowl and stir to combine. Add the tempeh and toss to coat.

Put the oil in the skillet. Add the tempeh, onion, carrots, bell pepper, celery, and any remaining seasoned flour. Cook, stirring occasionally, until the tempeh is browned, about 4 minutes. Stir in the chickpeas and garlic and cook, stirring occasionally, until fragrant, about 3 minutes. Add the tomatoes and their juice, water, lemon juice, and thyme and stir to combine. Let simmer, stirring occasionally, while you prepare the biscuits.

To make the biscuits and assemble the dish, put the flour, parsley, baking powder, and salt in a medium bowl and whisk to combine.

Put the soy milk, oil, agave nectar, and harissa paste in a small bowl and stir until well combined. Pour into the flour mixture and stir to make a smooth batter, with no streaks of flour remaining. The batter should be slightly dry.

Spoon the batter on the stew in 8 spoonfuls, spreading it slightly rather than mounding it so the biscuits will cook more evenly.

Close the lid and cook until the biscuits look dry on top and are golden brown, about 20 minutes. Serve each portion of stew topped with a biscuit.

1 (15-ounce) can low-sodium
   diced tomatoes, with juice

1 cup water

Juice from ½ lemon

½ teaspoon dried thyme

Harissa Biscuits

1½ cups all-purpose flour

3 tablespoons minced
   fresh parsley

1 tablespoon baking powder

½ teaspoon salt

½ cup unsweetened soy milk

3 tablespoons olive oil

1 tablespoon agave nectar

1 tablespoon harissa
   paste, homemade (page
   160) or store-bought

Indoor Method

Preheat the oven to 400 degrees F.

Prepare the stew in a large ovenproof skillet on the stove over medium-high heat as directed. Prepare and distribute the biscuit batter as directed. Put the skillet in the oven and bake for about 15 minutes, until the biscuits look dry on top and are golden brown. Serve as directed.

Per serving: 306 calories, 13 g protein, 11 g fat (2 g sat), 43 g carbs, 461 mg sodium, 138 mg calcium, 6 g fiber

Spanish in origin, paella was originally cooked over an open fire, making it a natural for this book. This recipe is far easier to make than it might appear from the ingredient list, and most of the preparation can be done in advance. If you're looking for the ultimate grilled dish for a dinner party, you've just found it.

PORCINI AND SAUSAGE PAELLA

Yield: 8 servings ● *Advance prep: Make Tangy Tofu Triangles (page 81; marinate but do not grill them).*

1 ounce dried porcini
   mushrooms

Generous pinch saffron
   threads, crumbled

3 cups boiling water

Salt-free vegetable
   broth, if needed

3 tablespoons olive oil

1¼ cups minced onion

7 ounces vegan
   sausage, chopped

1 tablespoon minced
   jalapeño chile

3 cloves garlic, minced

1½ cups arborio rice

2 teaspoons ground cumin

1 teaspoon ground coriander

1 teaspoon smoked paprika

Put the mushrooms and saffron in a medium bowl. Pour in the water and let rest for 20 minutes to rehydrate.

Drain the mushrooms, reserving the liquid. Strain the liquid through a coffee filter or several layers of cheesecloth to remove any grit. Measure out 2½ cups of the mushroom soaking liquid; if necessary, add salt-free vegetable broth to bring the amount up to 2½ cups. Discard any excess mushroom soaking liquid. Chop the mushrooms.

Outdoor Method

Preheat an outdoor grill to medium-high heat.

Put a 12-inch cast-iron skillet on the grill. Put the oil in the skillet and add the onion, sausage, chile, and garlic. Cook, stirring occasionally, until the onion is translucent, about 6 minutes. Add the rice, cumin, coriander, and paprika and cook, stirring frequently, for 1 to 2 minutes to lightly toast the rice and spices. Add the mushrooms, reserved mushroom soaking liquid, tomatoes, wine, parsley, and thyme. Stir to incorporate but don't stir again.

The grill should remain at medium-high heat until the dish is done (see Cook Smart); if the grill gets too hot, the paella may dry out. If it does become too hot, open the grill for a few minutes to release some heat.

Cook until the rice is tender and the bottom of the paella is toasted, 20 to 25 minutes; if the paella seems too dry during cooking, add additional broth, 1 tablespoon at a time, but don't stir it in. Remove from the heat.

Lightly oil the grill with canola oil. Put the tofu on the grill, reserving the marinade. Cook until marked, about 5 minutes,

1 (15-ounce) can low-
  sodium diced fire-roasted
  tomatoes with garlic

½ cup dry white wine or
  salt-free vegetable broth

3 tablespoons minced
  fresh parsley

1 tablespoon minced fresh
  thyme, or 1 teaspoon dried

1 pound Tangy Tofu Triangles
  (page 81), marinated
  but not grilled

1 red bell pepper, cut into
  ½-inch-thick rings

1 green bell pepper, cut
  into ½-inch-thick rings

1 lemon, cut into 8 wedges

occasionally basting with the marinade. Turn over and cook in the same fashion until the other side is marked, about 5 minutes.

Put the bell peppers on the grill and cook until marked, 3 to 4 minutes. Turn over and cook until the other side is marked, 2 to 3 minutes. Put the lemon wedges on the grill with one cut side down and cook until marked, about 4 minutes.

To serve, arrange the tofu triangles in a circle around the edge of the paella, overlapping them. Put the bell peppers in the center and arrange the lemon wedges on top of the tofu. Serve at once, letting diners squeeze lemon juice over their own servings if desired.

Indoor Method

Move a rack to the lowest position in the oven. Preheat the oven to 375 degrees F.

Prepare the rice mixture in a 12-inch ovenproof skillet on the stove over medium-high heat as directed. After adding the mushrooms, reserved mushroom soaking liquid, tomatoes, wine, parsley, and thyme, cover and bake for about 30 minutes, until the rice is dry on top and browned on the bottom.

Preheat a grill pan to medium-high heat.

Lightly oil the grill pan with canola oil. Cook the tofu, bell peppers, and lemon as directed. Serve as directed.

Per serving: 404 calories, 20 g protein, 15 g fat (2 g sat), 44 g carbs, 314 mg sodium, 237 mg calcium, 5 g fiber

Cook Smart

- If you are using a thermometer in the grill, aim for a temperature between 375 and 400 degrees F.

Chapter 5
Super Side Dishes

Fresh cucumbers combine with smoky grilled onion and fresh herbs and spices for a zippy yet cooling side dish.

SPICY ASIAN CUCUMBER SALAD

Yield: 4 servings

2 medium cucumbers, peeled and cut into ¼-inch-thick rounds

½ cup chopped grilled red onion (see page 14)

3 tablespoons seasoned rice vinegar

1 tablespoon mirin

1 teaspoon toasted sesame oil

1 teaspoon sriracha sauce

1 teaspoon reduced-sodium tamari

1 teaspoon minced fresh chives, or ¼ teaspoon dried

1 clove garlic, minced

½ teaspoon minced fresh mint

¼ teaspoon grated fresh ginger

¼ teaspoon red pepper flakes

¼ teaspoon salt

Pinch ground pepper

Put the cucumbers and onion in a medium bowl. Stir to combine.

Put the vinegar, mirin, oil, sriracha sauce, tamari, chives, garlic, mint, ginger, red pepper flakes, salt, and pepper in a small bowl and whisk to combine. Drizzle over the cucumbers and onion and stir gently to combine. Cover and refrigerate for at least 30 minutes before serving to allow the flavors to meld. Stored in a covered container in the refrigerator, the salad will keep for 3 days.

Per serving: 60 calories, 1 g protein, 1 g fat (0.2 g sat), 11 g carbs, 259 mg sodium, 72 mg calcium, 1 g fiber

This zesty slaw, which is enhanced by the addition of grilled sweet corn, is a favorite among vegans and nonvegans alike. Be prepared to share the recipe. Hope (or plan) for leftovers, as this slaw is used for Mexican Seitan Sandwiches (page 59).

MEXICAN SLAW

Yield: 8 servings • Advance prep: Make Roasted Corn on the Cob (page 130).

7 cups shredded green cabbage

Kernels from 3 ears Roasted Corn on the Cob (page 130; also see Cook Smart)

1 cup shredded carrot

1 cup minced scallions

½ cup finely chopped red bell pepper

½ cup vegan mayonnaise

2 tablespoons distilled white vinegar

Juice from 1 lime

1 chipotle chile in adobo sauce

½ teaspoon smoked paprika

¼ teaspoon ground pepper

Salt (optional)

Put the cabbage, corn, carrot, scallions, and bell pepper in a large bowl and stir to combine.

Put the vegan mayonnaise, vinegar, lime juice, chile, paprika, and pepper in a small blender or small bowl and process or whisk until smooth. Pour over the cabbage mixture and stir to combine. Season with salt to taste if desired. The slaw can be served immediately or stored in a covered container in the refrigerator for up to 2 days.

Per serving: 169 calories, 3 g protein, 9 g fat (1 g sat), 18 g carbs, 137 mg sodium, 33 mg calcium, 4 g fiber

Cook Smart

- If fresh corn is out of season, you can substitute frozen corn kernels. Put the corn in a dry cast-iron skillet over medium-high heat and cook, stirring occasionally, until browned, about 8 minutes.
- For a slightly sweeter slaw, add 1 to 2 teaspoons of agave nectar to the vegan mayonnaise mixture.

Grilling radicchio brings out its sweeter side, and pairing it with an Asian dressing balances its assertive flavor.

GRILLED RADICCHIO SALAD

See photo facing page 140.

Yield: 4 servings

1 head radicchio

2 heads baby bok choy, chopped

½ cup minced scallions

1 carrot, shredded

2 tablespoons reduced-sodium tamari

1½ tablespoons agave nectar

¼ teaspoon mirin

¼ teaspoon toasted sesame oil

Preheat a grill or grill pan to medium heat.

Lightly oil the grill with canola oil. Lightly mist the radicchio with olive oil spray. If using an outdoor grill, put the intact head of radicchio on the grill and close the lid. If using a grill pan, put the head of radicchio on the pan and cover with an inverted heatproof bowl to create an oven effect. Cook until marked and softened, about 6 minutes.

When the radicchio is cool enough to handle, quarter it and remove the core. Chop the radicchio and put it in a medium bowl. Add the bok choy, scallions, carrot, tamari, agave nectar, mirin, and oil and stir to combine. Serve warm or at room temperature.

Per serving: 67 calories, 3 g protein, 1 g fat (0.2 g sat), 13 g carbs, 401 mg sodium, 61 mg calcium, 2 g fiber

Many people don't know lettuce can be grilled, but here is delicious proof that it can be. Lemon, which is always a refreshing accent, appears here in the form of lemon pepper.

ROMAINE AND ASPARAGUS SALAD

Yield: 4 servings

2 tablespoons olive oil

¼ teaspoon salt

Pinch ground pepper

2 heads romaine lettuce, cut in half lengthwise, ends intact

6 ounces asparagus, trimmed

2 teaspoons reduced-sodium tamari

2 teaspoons balsamic vinegar

1 teaspoon lemon pepper

1 teaspoon maple syrup

2 tablespoons toasted pine nuts, chopped

1 tablespoon minced fresh chives

Preheat a grill, grill pan, or electric grill to medium-high heat.

Lightly oil the grill with canola oil. Put 1 tablespoon of the olive oil in a 13 x 9-inch baking pan. Sprinkle the salt and pepper evenly over the oil. Put the lettuce in the oil cut-side down to lightly coat it with the oil and seasonings. Then put the lettuce on the grill cut-side down and cook until lightly marked and softened, about 2 minutes (see Cook Smart). (If using an electric grill, keep it open for all of the vegetables and cook a few minutes longer if necessary.)

Put the asparagus in the baking pan and toss to coat with the oil remaining in the pan. Put the asparagus on the grill and cook until lightly marked and tender, about 8 minutes.

Chop the lettuce, discarding the end, and put it in a large bowl. When the asparagus is cool enough to handle, cut it into 1-inch pieces and add it to the bowl.

Put the remaining tablespoon of oil and the tamari, vinegar, lemon pepper, and maple syrup in a small bowl and stir to combine. Drizzle over the lettuce and asparagus, add the pine nuts and chives, and toss to coat. Serve warm or at room temperature.

Per serving: 158 calories, 6 g protein, 10 g fat (1 g sat), 15 g carbs, 373 mg sodium, 133 mg calcium, 7 g fiber

Cook Smart

- The tips of the lettuce will cook more quickly than the rest of the lettuce. Put the top end on a cooler part of the grill if possible. If the tips burn, cut them off and discard.

Zesty and full of fresh flavors, this salad is also as pretty as a summer day. The grilled corn and creamy avocado take humble black beans to a new level.

AVOCADO-CORN SALAD

Yield: 6 servings • *Advance prep: Make Roasted Corn on the Cob (page 130).*

Kernels from 4 ears Roasted Corn on the Cob (page 130; also see Cook Smart)

¾ cup minced scallions

½ red bell pepper, chopped

⅓ cup distilled white vinegar

2 tablespoons minced chipotle chiles in adobo sauce

2 teaspoons ground cumin

5 teaspoons olive oil

½ teaspoon ground white pepper

1 tablespoon minced fresh oregano, or 1 teaspoon dried

1 (15-ounce) can black beans, drained and rinsed

Salt (optional)

2 tablespoons freshly squeezed lemon juice

3 avocados, chilled (see Cook Smart)

Minced fresh cilantro, for garnish

Put the corn, scallions, and bell pepper in a large bowl and stir to combine.

Put the vinegar, chiles, and cumin in a small blender and process until smooth. Add 3 teaspoons of the oil and the white pepper and process again. Pour over the corn mixture. Add the oregano and stir to combine. Add the beans and stir gently so the beans don't break apart. Season with salt to taste if desired. Cover and refrigerate.

Preheat a grill, grill pan, or electric grill to medium heat.

Put the remaining 2 teaspoons of oil and the lemon juice in a small bowl. Stir to combine. Cut the avocados in half, remove the pits, and, using a large spoon, carefully scoop out the flesh, keeping the halves intact. Cut each half into 3 slices and brush with the lemon juice mixture.

Oil the grill with canola oil, using a little more oil than usual, as avocados are prone to sticking. Put the avocado slices on the grill and cook until marked, about 3 minutes. Carefully turn them over and cook until the other side is marked, about 2 minutes. (If using an electric grill, keep it open and cook a few minutes longer if necessary.)

To serve, divide the corn mixture among six plates and top each serving with 3 avocado slices. Garnish with cilantro and serve at room temperature.

Per serving: 316 calories, 10 g protein, 17 g fat (3 g sat), 39 g carbs, 267 mg sodium, 52 mg calcium, 12 g fiber

Cook Smart

- In a pinch, you can substitute 3 cups of frozen corn kernels for the grilled corn. Quickly rinse the frozen corn in hot water to thaw it and remove any lingering freezer taste, then drain it well.
- Refrigerate the avocados before cooking them on the grill. Avocados hold their shape better when cold.

Grilled potatoes, crisp on the outside and creamy in the middle, are combined with crunchy bell peppers and chile-infused mayonnaise to create an out-of-this-world side dish.

SPICY RED POTATO AND BELL PEPPER SALAD

Yield: 4 servings ● Advance prep: Make Roasted Garlic (page 20).

2 pounds small red potatoes, scrubbed

Olive oil

2 bell peppers, any color, chopped

½ cup chopped celery

½ cup chopped scallions

1 tablespoon cider vinegar

½ teaspoon salt

¼ teaspoon ground pepper

2 roasted poblano chiles (see page 14)

½ cup vegan mayonnaise

Juice from ½ lime

2 cloves Roasted Garlic (page 20)

¼ teaspoon chipotle chile powder

Bring a large pot of water to a boil over high heat. Add the potatoes, decrease the heat to medium-high, and cook until fork-tender, about 15 minutes. Drain well.

When the potatoes are cool enough to handle, cut them in half with a serrated knife and lightly brush the cut sides with olive oil.

Preheat a grill, grill pan, or electric grill to medium-high heat.

Put the potatoes on the grill cut-side down and cook until marked and slightly crisp, about 6 minutes. (If using an electric grill, keep it open and cook a few minutes longer if necessary.)

When the potatoes are cool enough to handle, cut them into 1-inch pieces and put them in a large bowl. Add the bell peppers, celery, and scallions and stir gently to combine. Drizzle with the vinegar and sprinkle with the salt and pepper. Stir gently to combine.

Put the chiles, vegan mayonnaise, lime juice, garlic, and chile powder in a small blender and process until smooth. Pour over the potato mixture and stir gently until the potatoes are evenly coated. The salad can be served immediately or stored in a covered container in the refrigerator for up to 2 days.

Per serving: 372 calories, 6 g protein, 18 g fat (1 g sat), 43 g carbs, 502 mg sodium, 50 mg calcium, 6 g fiber

Note: Analysis doesn't include olive oil for brushing the potatoes.

Cook Smart

• If you're a fan of spicy foods, try adding a roasted jalapeño chile to the dressing for even more heat.

Let others bring the macaroni salad to picnics and barbecues. You can take this barley-based salad, which has wonderful texture and Mediterranean flair.

LEMONY GREEK BARLEY SALAD

Yield: 4 servings • *Advance prep: Soak the barley for 2 hours.*

1 cup pearl barley, soaked in 2 cups water for 2 hours and drained (see Cook Smart)

½ red onion, cut into ¼-inch-thick rounds

½ green bell pepper, cut in half lengthwise

1 cup spinach, lightly packed and sliced

¼ cup chopped black olives

¼ cup minced moist-packed sun-dried tomatoes

1 tablespoon minced fresh parsley

3 tablespoons freshly squeezed lemon juice

2 tablespoons olive oil

2 tablespoons red wine vinegar

1 teaspoon dried oregano

½ teaspoon dried thyme

Salt (optional)

Ground pepper

Put about 4 cups of water in a medium saucepan and bring to a boil over high heat. Stir in the barley. Decrease the heat to low and simmer uncovered until tender, about 15 minutes. Drain. Rinse under cold water to stop the cooking and drain well. Put the barley in a large bowl.

Preheat a grill, grill pan, or electric grill to medium heat.

Lightly mist the grill with cooking spray. Put the onion and pepper on the grill. Cook until marked, about 5 minutes. (If using an electric grill, keep it open and cook a few minutes longer if necessary.)

When the onion and pepper are cool enough to handle, chop them and add them to the barley. Stir in the spinach, olives, sun-dried tomatoes, and parsley.

Put the lemon juice, oil, vinegar, oregano, and thyme in a small bowl and whisk to combine. Pour the dressing over the salad and stir to coat. Season with salt if desired, and pepper to taste. Cover and refrigerate for 1 hour to allow the flavors to meld.

Per serving: 308 calories, 7 g protein, 10 g fat (1 g sat), 50 g carbs, 140 mg sodium, 61 mg calcium, 12 g fiber

Note: Analysis doesn't include salt and ground pepper to taste.

Cook Smart

- Soaking the barley reduces the cooking time. Not only is this a welcome technique in hot weather (just be sure to soak the grain in the refrigerator), it's also environmentally friendly because it saves energy. This trick works with other grains too.
- If desired, substitute 3 cups cooked bulgur, quinoa, or Israeli couscous for the soaked and cooked barley.
- To make this a main dish, add 1 (15-ounce) can drained and rinsed chickpeas when you add the spinach.

This recipe makes a big batch, which is a good thing, because the dish is such a crowd-pleaser. Slathered in flavorful, fat-free Roasted Garlic Dressing and upscaled with artichoke hearts, bean salad has never had it so good. For a terrific meal, serve it alongside BBQ Portobello Grillers (page 72).

ITALIAN BEAN AND ORZO SALAD

Yield: 8 servings ● *Advance prep: Make Roasted Garlic Dressing (page 176).*

1 cup orzo

2 teaspoons olive oil

½ red onion, cut into ½-inch-thick rounds

1 red bell pepper, cut into ½-inch-thick rings

4 artichoke hearts packed in water, drained, patted dry, and cut into ½-inch pieces

1 (15-ounce) can black beans, drained and rinsed

1 (15-ounce) can chickpeas, drained and rinsed

1 (15-ounce) can red kidney beans, drained and rinsed

1 cup chopped celery

¼ cup chopped pepperoncini (optional)

¾ cup Roasted Garlic Dressing (page 176)

Bring a medium pot of water to a boil over high heat. Add the orzo, decrease the heat to medium-high, and cook, stirring occasionally, until tender but still firm, about 7 minutes. Drain and rinse under cold water. Put the orzo in a large bowl, drizzle with the oil, and stir gently until evenly coated to minimize sticking.

Preheat a grill, grill pan, or electric grill to medium-high heat.

Lightly oil the grill with canola oil. Put the onion on the grill and cook until marked, about 5 minutes. Put the bell pepper and artichokes on the grill and cook until marked, about 3 minutes.

When the onion, bell pepper, and artichokes are cool enough to handle, chop them and put them in the bowl with the orzo. Add the black beans, chickpeas, kidney beans, celery, and optional pepperoncini and stir gently to combine. Pour the dressing over the mixture and stir again. Cover and refrigerate for at least 1 hour to allow the flavors to meld. Stored in a covered container in the refrigerator the salad will keep for 3 days.

Per serving: 238 calories, 12 g protein, 2 g fat (0.2 g sat), 43 g carbs, 397 mg sodium, 79 mg calcium, 10 g fiber

In this recipe, roasted ears of corn, a Midwestern favorite, are enhanced with two seasoned butters: Chipotle Butter and Basil-Caper Butter. The only vegetable that rivals corn for superlative peak-of-season flavor has to be tomatoes. For a light summer meal, fill your plate with sliced tomatoes and an ear (or two!) of corn.

ROASTED CORN ON THE COB
WITH FLAVORED BUTTERS

Yield: 6 servings

Corn

6 ears corn on the cob, husks on

Chipotle Butter

3 tablespoons vegan margarine, at room temperature

1½ teaspoons minced chipotle chile in adobo sauce

¼ teaspoon salt

Basil-Caper Butter

3 tablespoons vegan margarine, at room temperature

1½ teaspoons minced fresh basil

¾ teaspoon minced capers

Cook Smart

- Grill extra corn for quick meals later in the week. Kernels cut from the cobs are especially good in tofu scrambles or for Avocado-Corn Salad (page 126).

To prepare the corn, remove most of the husks, leaving just the last few layers surrounding the kernels and keeping them attached to the stalk. If time permits, soak the corn in cold water for 40 minutes; this will provide extra moisture as the corn cooks.

To make the chipotle butter and the basil-caper butter, put all the ingredients for each butter in seperate small bowls and mix well. Cover and refrigerate until serving time.

The butters can be used immediately or may be stored in covered containers in the refrigerator for up to 1 week.

Outdoor Method

Preheat an outdoor grill to medium heat.

Put the corn on the grill and close the lid. Cook, turning occasionally, until marked all over and the shape of the kernels is visible through the husks, about 30 minutes. The corn can be used or eaten immediately or may be stored in a ziplock bag in the refrigerator for up to 4 days. Serve with the flavored butters.

Indoor Method

Preheat the oven to 350 degrees F. Put the corn directly on the oven rack and bake for about 30 minutes, turning once, until the kernels become visible through the husks. Store or serve as directed.

Per serving (with Chipotle Butter): 174 calories, 5 g protein, 8 g fat (3 g sat), 27 g carbs, 175 mg sodium, 2 mg calcium, 4 g fiber

Per serving (with Basil-Caper Butter): 173 calories, 5 g protein, 8 g fat (3 g sat), 27 g carbs, 77 mg sodium, 2 mg calcium, 4 g fiber

After years of making this side dish in the oven, I discovered that it's even better grilled. Cutting the cauliflower in half helps it cook more quickly, but the cooking time can still vary depending on the cauliflower—and depending on your preference. Longer cooking will result in a sweeter flavor.

GARLICKY CAULIFLOWER

Yield: 4 servings

10 cloves garlic, peeled

1 head cauliflower, cut in half vertically

2 tablespoons vegan margarine, at room temperature, or olive oil

¼ teaspoon salt

⅛ teaspoon ground pepper

Outdoor Method

Preheat an outdoor grill to medium-high heat.

Wedge the whole garlic cloves into gaps between the cauliflower florets. If necessary, use a paring knife to cut small holes for the garlic. Spread 1 tablespoon of the margarine over the entire surface of each cauliflower half and sprinkle with the salt and pepper. Wrap each cauliflower half separately in foil.

Put the cauliflower on the grill and cook until fork-tender, about 20 minutes. Turn over and cook until the other side is fork-tender, about 20 minutes. Cut each half in half to serve.

Indoor Method

Preheat the oven to 400 degrees F. Prepare and wrap the cauliflower as directed and bake for about 40 minutes, until fork-tender.

Per serving: 108 calories, 4 g protein, 5 g fat (0.2 g sat), 14 g carbs, 248 mg sodium, 45 mg calcium, 5 g fiber

Cook Smart

- You can easily adapt the seasonings in this recipe to coordinate with the other dishes that you're serving. For example, use fewer cloves of garlic and rub either 1 teaspoon of curry powder or 1 teaspoon of chili powder over the cauliflower before sprinkling with the salt and pepper.

This grilled version of a traditional French recipe is sure to become a summer favorite. Full of the best of summer's vegetables, the ratatouille becomes a meal when ladled over couscous or rice or accompanied by crusty bread. It's very adaptable, so feel free to substitute your favorite vegetables or those that are in season. If you're lucky enough to have leftovers, use them for Portobellos Smothered in Grilled Ratatouille (page 97) or Open-Faced Ratatouille Sandwiches (page 55).

GRILLED RATATOUILLE

Yield: 4 servings ● *Advance prep: Make Roasted Garlic (page 20).*

2 cups (1 pint) cherry tomatoes, halved

1 tablespoon olive oil

1 tablespoon minced fresh thyme, or 1 teaspoon dried

½ teaspoon ground pepper

½ teaspoon herbes de Provence

1 eggplant, cut lengthwise into ½-inch-thick slabs

1 summer squash, cut lengthwise into ½-inch-thick slabs

1 zucchini, cut lengthwise into ½-inch-thick slabs

1 onion, cut into ½-inch-thick rounds

1 red bell pepper, quartered, or cut into rings if cooking indoors

½ cup minced fresh basil

Outdoor Method

Preheat an outdoor grill to medium-high heat.

Put the tomatoes, oil, dried thyme (if using), pepper, and herbes de Provence in a deep 13 x 9-inch foil roasting pan and stir to combine. Put the roasting pan on the grill and close the lid. Cook, stirring the mixture occasionally, until the tomatoes have some charred spots, about 12 minutes. Remove from the heat.

Lightly mist the eggplant, squash, zucchini, onion, and bell pepper with olive oil spray. Put them on the grill and cook until marked, 4 to 5 minutes. Turn over and cook until the other side is marked and the vegetables are tender but not soft, 4 to 5 minutes.

When the grilled vegetables are cool enough to handle, chop them and add them to the tomato mixture. Add the basil, garlic, parsley, vinegar, wine, and fresh thyme (if using). Put the pan back on the grill and cook, stirring occasionally, for 10 minutes to allow the flavors to meld. Season with salt to taste if desired. Serve hot or at room temperature.

6 cloves Roasted Garlic
(page 20), minced

2 tablespoons minced fresh
parsley

2 tablespoon balsamic vinegar

2 tablespoons dry red wine or
salt-free vegetable broth

Salt (optional)

Indoor Method

Preheat the oven to 400 degrees F.

Put the tomatoes, oil, dried thyme (if using), pepper, and herbes de Provence in a deep 13 x 9-inch nonreactive baking pan and stir to combine. Bake for about 25 minutes, until the tomatoes have some charred spots.

Preheat a grill pan or electric grill to medium-high heat.

Grill the vegetables as directed. (If using an electric grill, keep it open and cook a few minutes longer if necessary.) Assemble the dish as directed and return to the oven for 15 minutes. Serve hot or at room temperature.

Per serving: 145 calories, 3 g protein, 5 g fat (1 g sat), 19 g carbs, 46 mg sodium, 47 mg calcium, 8 g fiber

Baby bok choy, a menu staple at Chinese restaurants, gets the grill treatment here—to delicious effect!

BABY BOK CHOY WITH SESAME SEEDS

Yield: 4 servings

2 teaspoons toasted sesame oil

2 teaspoons reduced-sodium tamari

1 teaspoon toasted sesame seeds

¼ teaspoon five-spice powder

2 heads baby bok choy, cut in half lengthwise

Preheat a grill, grill pan, or electric grill to medium-high heat.

Lightly oil the grill with canola oil. Put the oil, tamari, sesame seeds, and five-spice powder in a small bowl and stir to combine. Lightly brush the mixture on the cut sides of the bok choy. Put the bok choy on the grill cut-side down and cook until marked, about 5 minutes, basting occasionally with any remaining oil mixture. Turn over and cook in the same fashion until the other side is marked, about 3 minutes. (If using an electric grill, keep it open and cook a few minutes longer if necessary.)

Per serving: 30 calories, 1 g protein, 3 g fat (0.3 g sat), 1 g carbs, 138 mg sodium, 35 mg calcium, 0 g fiber

Cook Smart

- Use the oil mixture in this recipe as a marinade for skewered sugar snap peas, snow peas, or asparagus stalks. Grill the vegetables until bright green and marked.

Cutting the potatoes as thinly as possible helps them absorb the seasonings, and cooking them in foil seals in the flavors.

SMOKY PACKET POTATOES

Yield: 4 servings

1 pound small red potatoes, scrubbed and cut into thin rounds

1 tablespoon minced fresh chives, or 1 teaspoon dried

1 tablespoon olive oil

2 teaspoons nutritional yeast flakes

1 teaspoon liquid smoke

¼ teaspoon paprika

¼ teaspoon salt

Pinch ground pepper

Outdoor Method

Preheat an outdoor grill to medium-high heat. Tear off one 24-inch piece of foil. Lightly mist the foil with cooking spray.

Put all the ingredients in a medium bowl and stir gently until the potatoes are evenly coated. Spread the potatoes on the foil in a thin layer, no deeper than 1 inch, to help ensure even cooking. Wrap the foil around the potatoes, making a disk-shaped packet. Put the packet on the grill and cook for 10 minutes. Turn over and cook until the potatoes are tender and golden, about 8 minutes. (You will need to open the packet to check for doneness.)

Indoor Method

Preheat an electric grill fitted with the smooth plates to high heat.

Prepare and wrap the potatoes as directed. Put the packet on the grill, close the lid, and cook until the potatoes are tender and golden, about 30 minutes. Alternatively, preheat the oven to 400 degrees F and bake the packet for 25 to 30 minutes, until the potatoes are tender and golden.

Per serving: 114 calories, 2 g protein, 4 g fat (1 g sat), 18 g carbs, 152 mg sodium, 11 mg calcium, 2 g fiber

Testers who made these hash browns on an electric grill swore that they were the best hash browns they'd ever tasted. As an added bonus, they're lower in fat than typical stovetop hash browns. That said, preparing them in a cast-iron skillet also yields good results, but it does require extra oil.

OH-SO-EASY HASH BROWNS

Yield: 4 servings

1½ pounds russet potatoes, scrubbed

½ cup minced onion

1 to 3 tablespoons canola oil

½ teaspoon paprika

½ teaspoon salt

¼ teaspoon ground pepper

Shred the potatoes using a food processor or grater. Spin them dry in a salad spinner or squeeze as much moisture out of them as possible by wrapping them in a clean, lint-free kitchen towel and twisting the ends. The drier the potatoes are, the crisper the hash browns will be. Put the potatoes and onion in a large bowl. Drizzle with 1 tablespoon of the oil and sprinkle with the paprika, salt, and pepper. Stir gently until the potatoes are evenly coated.

Electric Grill Method

Preheat the oven to 300 degrees F. Preheat an electric grill fitted with the smooth plates to medium-high heat.

Lightly mist the grill with cooking spray. Spoon half of the potatoes onto the grill, spreading them smoothly to the edges in a thin layer. Close the lid and cook until golden and crisp, about 6 minutes. Transfer the potatoes to an ovenproof platter and keep warm in the oven while cooking the remaining potatoes in the same fashion.

Outdoor Grill or Stovetop Method

Preheat an outdoor grill to medium heat and put a large cast-iron skillet on the grill. Alternatively, put the skillet on the stovetop over medium-high heat.

Put the remaining 2 tablespoons of canola oil in the skillet. When the oil is hot, add the potatoes. Pat them into an even layer with the back of a turner. If cooking on the stovetop, decrease the heat to medium. Cook the potatoes until golden and crisp, about 7 minutes. Turn over in sections and cook until the other side is golden, about 5 minutes.

Per serving: 129 calories, 3 g protein, 5 g fat (0.3 g sat), 21 g carbs, 190 mg sodium, 18 mg calcium, 2 g fiber

Think of this dish, seasoned with the Ethiopian spice blend berberé, as baked beans with superpowers. If canned fava beans and lentils aren't available, substitute chickpeas and Great Northern beans or navy beans; the chickpeas are firmer, like fava beans, and the white beans are more tender, like lentils. To turn this into a main dish, serve the beans with crusty bread and a green salad.

ETHIOPIAN BEAN SKILLET

Yield: 6 servings

1 leek, white part only (about 4 inches), washed well (see Cook Smart, page 29)

1 tablespoon olive oil

½ green bell pepper, roasted (see page 14) and chopped

¼ cup minced carrot

¼ teaspoon ground pepper

Pinch salt

1 tablespoon grated fresh ginger

2 cloves garlic, minced

1 teaspoon berberé (see Cook Smart)

1 teaspoon ground cumin

1 teaspoon smoked paprika

¼ teaspoon ground cayenne

1 (15-ounce) can fava beans, drained and rinsed

1 (15-ounce) can lentils, drained and rinsed

1 cup salt-free vegetable broth

1 tablespoon no-salt-added tomato paste

2 teaspoons cider vinegar

1 teaspoon molasses

Juice from ½ lemon

Preheat a grill, grill pan, or electric grill to medium-high heat.

Lightly oil the grill with canola oil. Put the leek on the grill and cook until marked, about 5 minutes. Turn over and cook until the other side is marked, about 5 minutes. (If using an electric grill, keep it open and cook a few minutes longer if necessary.)

When the leek is cool enough to handle, slice it thinly. Heat the oil in a large cast-iron skillet on an outdoor grill or on the stove over medium-high heat. Add the leek, bell pepper, carrot, pepper, and salt and cook, stirring occasionally, for 2 to 3 minutes. Add the ginger, garlic, *berberé*, cumin, paprika, and cayenne and cook, stirring constantly, for 1 minute to lightly toast the spices, being careful not to burn the garlic. Add the beans, lentils, broth, tomato paste, vinegar, and molasses and cook, stirring occasionally, until heated through and the flavors have melded, about 15 minutes. Stir in the lemon juice before serving.

Per serving: 135 calories, 6 g protein, 3 g fat (0.4 g sat), 20 g carbs, 354 mg sodium, 65 mg calcium, 5 g fiber

Cook Smart

• Berberé is an Ethiopian spice blend that typically contains chiles, garlic, and fenugreek, along with other spices. Look for it at African markets or in stores with a well-stocked spice section. The blend can vary considerably, so once the dish is cooked, taste and add more berberé if you wish.

Lower in fat than fast-food versions, these noodles are slightly spicy with a bit of crunchiness from being grilled. Testers were so excited about this recipe that they tried it with several different kinds of noodles. Soba noodles work well, as do gluten-free rice noodles. If you opt for gluten-free noodles, be careful not to overcook them.

ASIAN SESAME NOODLES

Yield: 4 servings

1 pound linguine

½ cup shredded carrot

¼ cup minced scallions

2 tablespoons toasted sesame seeds

2 cloves garlic, minced

2 tablespoons reduced-sodium tamari

5 teaspoons toasted sesame oil

1 tablespoon hot chile oil

½ teaspoon ground pepper

Salt (optional)

Bring a large pot of water to a boil over high heat. Add the linguine and decrease the heat to medium-high. Cook, stirring occasionally, until tender but still firm, about 10 minutes. Drain and rinse under cold water to stop the cooking. Drain again.

Put the noodles in a large bowl. Add the carrot, scallions, sesame seeds, and garlic and toss gently to combine. Drizzle with the tamari, sesame oil, and hot chile oil and sprinkle with the pepper. Season with salt to taste if desired. Toss gently until the noodles are evenly coated.

Electric Grill Method

Preheat the oven to 300 degrees F. Preheat an electric grill fitted with the smooth plates to high heat.

Lightly mist the grill with cooking spray. Spread half of the noodle mixture in an even layer on the grill. Close the lid and cook until crisp, about 9 minutes. Transfer the noodles to an ovenproof platter and keep warm in the oven while cooking the remaining noodles in the same fashion.

Outdoor Method

Preheat an outdoor grill to medium-low heat. Tear off two 18-inch pieces of foil.

Put the noodle mixture on the foil, dividing it evenly. Wrap the foil around the noodles, making disk-shaped packets. Put the packets on the grill and cook for about 8 minutes. Turn over and cook until the noodles are crisp, about 7 minutes. (You will need to open the packet to check for doneness.)

Per serving: 514 calories, 16 g protein, 12 g fat (1 g sat), 85 g carbs, 374 mg sodium, 46 mg calcium, 4 g fiber

Chapter 6

Delectable Desserts

All types of grapefruit are chock-full of vitamin C, but for maximum nutrition, choose a red or pink variety. This dish is a lovely, light dessert, and it can also provide a sweet start to any morning. Citrus is especially refreshing after a meal of Asian cuisine.

MAPLE-GLAZED GRAPEFRUIT

Yield: 4 servings

2 grapefruits

1 tablespoon maple syrup

½ teaspoon vanilla extract

Preheat a grill, grill pan, or electric grill to medium-high heat.

Cut the grapefruits in half crosswise. Use a sharp or serrated knife to cut along the edges of the membranes and the rim of the rind. This will make the sections easier to remove. Put the grapefruits on the grill cut-side down and cook for 5 to 7 minutes. The fruit may not develop grill marks, but the color of the pulp will darken slightly. (If using an electric grill, keep it open and cook a few minutes longer if necessary.)

Put the maple syrup and vanilla extract in a small bowl and stir to combine. Brush the mixture evenly on the cut side of the grapefruit halves. Serve the grapefruits warm.

Per serving: 63 calories, 1 g protein, 0 g fat (0 g sat), 16 g carbs, 0 mg sodium, 29 mg calcium, 2 g fiber

Grilled Radicchio Salad, p. 124

Skillet-Grilled Mango-Blueberry Cobbler, p. 147

Spiced and sweetened vegan cream cheese makes an ideal dip for fresh fruit. The dip must chill for at least one hour before serving. That makes for a leisurely dessert; when it's time to indulge, all you'll have to do is grill the fruit.

CREAMY CINNAMON-NUTMEG DIP
WITH FRUIT SKEWERS

Yield: 4 servings

Creamy Cinnamon-Nutmeg Dip

¼ cup plus 2 tablespoons vegan cream cheese, at room temperature

¼ cup vegan sour cream

1 tablespoon agave nectar

1 tablespoon maple syrup

½ teaspoon vanilla extract

⅛ teaspoon ground cinnamon

Pinch ground nutmeg

Fruit

12 fresh strawberries

12 fresh pineapple chunks

1 mango, peeled and cut into 12 equal-sized chunks (see Cook Smart)

To make the dip, put all the ingredients in a small bowl and whisk vigorously until smooth. Cover and refrigerate for at least 1 hour to allow the flavors to meld. The dip can be used immediately (after it has chilled) or may be stored in a covered container in the refrigerator for up to 1 week.

To prepare the fruit and serve, soak four wooden skewers in water for 30 minutes. Alternatively, lightly mist four metal skewers with cooking spray.

Preheat a grill, grill pan, or electric grill to medium heat.

Put the strawberries, pineapple, and mango on the skewers, alternating them. Mist with olive oil spray. Put the skewers on the grill and cook until marked, about 4 minutes. Turn over and cook until the other side is marked, about 3 minutes. (If using an electric grill, keep it open and cook a few minutes longer if necessary.)

Serve the skewers with the dip alongside.

Per serving: 377 calories, 3 g protein, 6 g fat (3 g sat), 74 g carbs, 172 mg sodium, 10 mg calcium, 2 g fiber

Cook Smart

• Cut the mango in half lengthwise, starting at the stem end and cutting around the fruit until you return to the stem end. Twist the halves in opposite directions and pry the mango apart. Using a knife or spoon, carefully remove the pit. Cut the flesh of each mango half two times lengthwise and three times crosswise, then carefully cut the flesh from the skin.

Delectable mangoes become even sweeter when grilled. Here, grilled mango is combined with fresh berries to create a dessert bursting with complex flavor. There will be a little leftover cinnamon sugar. Enjoy it on breakfast toast.

FRUIT SALSA WITH SWEET CINNAMON CHIPS

Yield: 4 servings

1 large mango, halved and pitted (see Cook Smart)

⅓ cup fresh blueberries

¼ cup chopped fresh strawberries

1 tablespoon freshly squeezed lemon juice

1 teaspoon minced fresh mint

1 tablespoon sugar

¼ teaspoon ground cinnamon

4 (8-inch) flour tortillas

1 tablespoon mild olive oil

Preheat a grill, grill pan, or electric grill to medium heat.

Put the mango on the grill cut-side down and cook until marked, about 5 minutes. (If using an electric grill, keep it open and cook a few minutes longer if necessary.)

When the mango is cool enough to handle, make perpendicular cuts across the flesh to form cubes. Cut the cubes from the skin and put them in a medium bowl. Add the blueberries, strawberries, lemon juice, and mint and stir gently to combine.

Preheat the oven to 400 degrees F.

Put the sugar and cinnamon in a small bowl and stir to combine. Brush one side of each tortilla with the oil and sprinkle with a generous ½ teaspoon of the sugar mixture. Cut each tortilla into six wedges. Put the pieces on a baking sheet and bake until lightly browned, about 4 minutes. The chips will crisp as they cool. The chips can be used immediately or may be stored in a covered container at room temperature for up to 2 days.

To serve, divide the mango mixture among four plates and surround it with the chips.

Per serving: 206 calories, 3 g protein, 7 g fat (2 g sat), 34 g carbs, 341 mg sodium, 29 mg calcium, 3 g fiber

Cook Smart

• Cut the mango in half lengthwise, starting at the stem end and cutting around the fruit until you return to the stem end. Twist the halves in opposite directions and pry the mango apart. Using a knife or spoon, carefully remove the pit.

It's not often that jalapeño chiles and basil are used in a dessert topping, but when they're combined with grilled apricots and white balsamic vinegar, the result is irresistible. Spoon this sauce generously over vegan vanilla ice cream or thick slices of fresh or lightly grilled pound cake.

SPICED APRICOT SAUCE

Yield: 6 servings

12 ounces apricots, halved and pitted (see Cook Smart)

½ lime

¼ jalapeño chile

2 tablespoons maple syrup

1 tablespoon white balsamic vinegar

Pinch salt

2 teaspoons minced fresh basil

Preheat a grill, grill pan, or electric grill to medium-high heat.

Lightly oil the grill with canola oil. Put the apricots on the grill cut-side down and, if using an outdoor grill, close the lid. Cook the apricots until marked, about 5 minutes. (If using an electric grill, keep it open for the apricots, lime, and chile and cook a few minutes longer if necessary.)

Put the lime and chile on the grill and cook until marked, about 3 minutes. (If using an outdoor grill, put the chile on a small piece of foil to keep it from falling through the grates.)

When the lime and chile are cool enough to handle, juice the lime and mince the chile. Put the apricots, lime juice, maple syrup, vinegar, and salt in a blender and process to make a smooth sauce. Transfer to a small bowl and stir in the basil and chile. The sauce can be used immediately or may be stored in a covered container in the refrigerator for up to 1 week.

Per serving: 49 calories, 0 g protein, 0 g fat (0 g sat), 12 g carbs, 26 mg sodium, 70 mg calcium, 2 g fiber

Cook Smart

- If fresh apricots aren't available, substitute 1 (15-ounce) can unsweetened apricots, drained.

Raspberries and peaches have been a classic combination since they were introduced as a couple in this elegant dessert at the Savoy Hotel in London around 1892. This version is updated with ancho chile powder and white balsamic vinegar.

PEACH MELBA

Yield: 4 servings

Raspberry Sauce

2 cups fresh raspberries

3 tablespoons freshly squeezed orange juice

1 tablespoon maple syrup

½ teaspoon ancho chile powder

1 tablespoon cold water

1 tablespoon cornstarch

Fruit and Topping

4 teaspoons white balsamic vinegar

2 teaspoons maple syrup

½ teaspoon ground cinnamon

4 peaches, peeled, halved, and pitted (see Cook Smart)

Vegan vanilla ice cream, for serving (optional)

½ cup raspberries, for garnish

Minced fresh mint leaves, for garnish

To make the sauce, put the raspberries, orange juice, maple syrup, and chile powder in a small saucepan and bring to a boil over medium heat. Decrease the heat to low and simmer uncovered, stirring occasionally, until the raspberries are broken down, 5 to 7 minutes.

Put the water and cornstarch in a small bowl and stir to form a slurry. Add to the raspberry mixture and cook, stirring constantly, until thickened, 2 to 3 minutes. The sauce can be used immediately or may be stored in a covered container in the refrigerator for up to 1 week.

To prepare the fruit and assemble the dish, preheat a grill, grill pan, or electric grill to medium heat.

Put the vinegar, maple syrup, and cinnamon in a small bowl and stir to make a glaze. Lightly oil the grill with canola oil. Brush the peaches with the glaze. Put them on the grill cut-side down and cook until marked, about 5 minutes, occasionally basting with the glaze. Turn over and cook in the same fashion until the other side is marked, about 5 minutes. (If using an electric grill, keep it open and cook a few minutes longer if necessary.)

Spoon the sauce onto four plates. Put 2 peach halves on each plate. Top with a scoop of vegan vanilla ice cream if desired. Garnish with the raspberries and mint.

Per serving: 162 calories, 3 g protein, 1 g fat (0 g sat), 35 g carbs, 32 mg sodium, 26 mg calcium, 9 g fiber

Note: Analysis doesn't include vegan vanilla ice cream for serving or fresh mint leaves for garnish.

Cook Smart

- Overly ripe peaches tend not to grill well. Just ripe or even slightly underripe peaches hold up better.
- To peel peaches easily, fill a medium saucepan halfway with water and bring to a boil over high heat. Fill a bowl with ice-cold water. Cut a small X in the bottom of each peach. Put the peaches in the boiling water and cook for 45 seconds or, if the peaches are slightly underripe, for 1 minute. Drain and plunge into the bowl of cold water. When the peaches are cool enough to handle, peel the skins off by hand.

The seasonings in the granola that tops this dessert make it unique. Five-spice powder and black pepper aren't usually the first ingredients that come to mind when you think of granola! When this flavor combination is paired with luscious grilled nectarines and creamy vegan ice cream, the results are spectacular. Think of this dessert as a deconstructed fruit crisp à la mode.

GRILLED NECTARINES WITH FIVE-SPICE GRANOLA

Yield: 4 servings

Five-Spice Granola

1 cup old-fashioned rolled oats

2 tablespoons blanched slivered almonds

¼ teaspoon five-spice powder

⅛ teaspoon ground ginger

Pinch salt

Pinch ground pepper

2 tablespoons canola oil

2 tablespoons maple syrup

1 tablespoon light brown sugar

1 teaspoon vanilla extract

Fruit and Topping

4 nectarines, halved and pitted (see Cook Smart)

1 cup vegan vanilla ice cream, or ½ cup vegan vanilla yogurt

To make the granola, preheat the oven to 300 degrees F. Line a 13 x 9-inch baking pan with parchment paper.

Put the oats, almonds, five-spice powder, ginger, salt, and pepper in a medium bowl and stir to combine.

Put the oil, maple syrup, brown sugar, and vanilla extract in a small bowl and stir to combine. Drizzle over the oat mixture and stir until evenly coated.

Spread the mixture evenly in the lined baking pan. Bake until golden, about 25 minutes, stirring every 10 minutes and being careful not to overbake, as the granola can burn easily. Let cool completely; the granola will crisp as it cools. The granola can be used immediately or may be stored in a covered container at room temperature for up to 3 weeks.

To prepare the fruit and assemble the dish, heat a grill, grill pan, or electric grill to medium-high heat.

Lightly oil the grill with canola oil. Put the nectarines on the grill cut-side down and cook until marked, about 3 minutes. (If using an electric grill, keep it open and cook a few minutes longer if necessary.)

To serve, put 2 nectarine halves on each plate, grilled-side up. Top each with the vegan ice cream. Sprinkle the granola over the ice cream and serve immediately.

Per serving: 372 calories, 6 g protein, 18 g fat (2 g sat), 54 g carbs, 54 mg sodium, 23 mg calcium, 6 g fiber

Cook Smart

- Overly ripe nectarines tend not to grill well. Just ripe or even slightly underripe nectarines hold up better.
- If it's difficult to remove the pits from the nectarines, cut them into quarters, rather than halves.
- You can substitute peaches or plums for the nectarines, or use several different stone fruits for a stunning presentation.

If pies are the quintessential American dessert, cobblers have to be a very close second. However, this one surpasses both by incorporating mangoes, basil, and cardamom for enticing and unusual flavor.

SKILLET-GRILLED MANGO-BLUEBERRY COBBLER

See photo facing page 141.

Yield: 4 servings

2 large mangoes, cut into 1-inch chunks (see Cook Smart, page 141)

1 cup fresh or frozen blueberries (see Cook Smart)

Juice from ½ lemon

2 tablespoons minced fresh basil

2 tablespoons maple syrup

2 teaspoons tapioca starch or cornstarch

½ teaspoon ground cinnamon

¼ teaspoon ground cardamom

¼ teaspoon plus 1 pinch salt

½ cup all-purpose flour

1 teaspoon baking powder

2 tablespoons mild olive oil

2 tablespoons plain soy milk

1 teaspoon vanilla extract

Preheat an outdoor grill to medium heat or preheat the oven to 375 degrees F.

Put the mangoes, blueberries, lemon juice, basil, 1 tablespoon of the maple syrup, and the tapioca starch, cinnamon, cardamom, and pinch of salt in an 8-inch cast-iron skillet. Stir to combine.

Put the flour, baking powder, and ¼ teaspoon of salt in a small bowl and stir to combine.

Put the oil, soy milk, the remaining teaspoon of the maple syrup, and the vanilla extract in a small bowl and whisk to combine. Pour into the flour mixture and stir to combine. Spoon the batter on top of the fruit in 4 spoonfuls, spreading it slightly rather than mounding it so it will cook more evenly.

Put the skillet on the grill and close the lid, or put the skillet in the oven. Cook until the biscuits are lightly golden, about 25 minutes.

Per serving: 236 calories, 3 g protein, 8 g fat (1 g sat), 44 g carbs, 225 mg sodium, 75 mg calcium, 4 g fiber

Cook Smart

• If the mangoes or blueberries you have are out of season or aren't very sweet, add another tablespoon of maple syrup to the fruit mixture.

Sour cherries are more tart than their sweet cherry cousins, such as Bing cherries. They are rarely eaten alone, as popping one in your mouth leads to a tantalizing but powerful pucker. Because cherries have a short season and are only available from late spring to early summer, cherry fans have to act quickly. But the good news is that they freeze wonderfully (see Cook Smart).

SKILLET-GRILLED CHERRY CRISP

Yield: 4 servings

4 cups pitted sour cherries (see Cook Smart)

¾ cup light brown sugar, lightly packed

¼ cup cornstarch

Grated zest from ½ lemon

¼ teaspoon grated fresh ginger

½ cup whole wheat pastry flour

¼ cup old-fashioned rolled oats

¼ cup panko breadcrumbs

¼ cup dark brown sugar, lightly packed

1 teaspoon ground cinnamon

Pinch salt

¼ cup canola oil

Vegan ice cream, for serving (optional)

Preheat an outdoor grill to medium heat or preheat the oven to 375 degrees F.

Put the cherries, light brown sugar, cornstarch, lemon zest, and ginger in a medium bowl and stir to combine. Pour into an 8-inch cast-iron skillet.

Put the flour, oats, breadcrumbs, dark brown sugar, cinnamon, and salt in a small bowl. Drizzle with the oil and mix well with a fork. Sprinkle evenly over the cherries.

Put the skillet on the grill and close the lid, or put the skillet in the oven. Cook until the top is crisp and the cherry mixture is bubbly, about 25 minutes. Serve warm or at room temperature, topped with vegan ice cream if desired.

Per serving: 566 calories, 4 g protein, 15 g fat (1 g sat), 113 g carbs, 104 mg sodium, 20 mg calcium, 4 g fiber

Note: Analysis doesn't include vegan ice cream for serving.

Cook Smart

- To freeze fresh cherries, wash and pit them, then spread them on a rimmed baking sheet. Put the baking sheet in the freezer. When the cherries are frozen solid, transfer them to a ziplock bag and return them to the freezer, where they will keep for about six months.
- If fresh cherries aren't available, frozen or drained canned cherries can be used. Be careful to buy sour cherries (sometimes called tart or pie cherries) rather than sweetened ones.

Incredibly easy but oh so delicious, these miniature pies with a tortilla crust will satisfy dessert cravings any time of day or night. Although lemon juice might be an unusual ingredient for caramel sauce, the acidity discourages sugar crystals from forming. For instant satisfaction, just make the caramel sauce and dip apple slices into it.

ALMOST-INSTANT APPLE PIES
WITH DARK CARAMEL SAUCE

Yield: 2 pies, 4 servings

Caramel Sauce

2 tablespoons vegan margarine

⅓ cup light brown sugar, firmly packed

1 tablespoon maple syrup

2 teaspoons plain soy milk

1 teaspoon freshly squeezed lemon juice

Pinch salt

Apple Pies

1 Granny Smith apple, peeled and diced

2 teaspoons freshly squeezed lemon juice

½ teaspoon ground cinnamon

4 (8-inch) flour tortillas

To make the sauce, melt the margarine in a small saucepan over low heat. Add the brown sugar, maple syrup, soy milk, lemon juice, and salt and whisk to combine. Increase the heat to medium-low. Heat, whisking constantly, until just barely bubbling; be careful not to overheat the sauce, as it can burn easily. Decrease the heat to low if necessary. Cook, whisking almost constantly, until the sauce is smooth and not at all grainy, 4 to 5 minutes. The sauce can be used immediately or may be stored in a covered container in the refrigerator for up to 4 days. If chilled, gently warm the sauce over low heat before using.

To make and serve the pies, preheat the oven to 200 degrees F. Fit an electric grill with the smooth plates and preheat to medium heat.

Put the apple, lemon juice, and cinnamon in a small bowl and gently toss to combine. Spread the mixture evenly over two of the tortillas. Cover with the remaining tortillas.

Put one of the pies on the grill and close the lid. Cook until lightly browned and crisp, about 8 minutes. Transfer to a plate and keep warm in the oven while cooking the second pie.

Cut each pie into quarters. Put 2 quarters on each plate and drizzle with the warm caramel sauce.

Per serving: 268 calories, 3 g protein, 9 g fat (4 g sat), 46 g carbs, 432 mg sodium, 35 mg calcium, 2 g fiber

Couscous, which hails from North Africa, has become widely popular. It's typically included in savory dishes. In Egypt, however, it's often served as a dessert, topped with a dollop of cream. This sweet couscous cake is a unique and intriguing way to end a meal.

PINEAPPLE AND POMEGRANATE COUSCOUS CAKES

Yield: 4 servings

1 cup water

2 tablespoons agave nectar

2 tablespoons pomegranate molasses

¼ teaspoon salt

1 cup couscous

4 slices fresh pineapple, about ½ inch thick

1 cup pomegranate seeds

Put the water, agave nectar, molasses, and salt in a small saucepan and stir to combine. Bring to a boil over medium-high heat. Stir in the couscous, cover, and remove from the heat. Let sit until the liquid is absorbed, 4 to 5 minutes. Fluff with a fork.

Preheat a grill, grill pan, or electric grill to medium heat.

Lightly oil the grill with canola oil. Put the pineapple on the grill and cook until marked, about 4 minutes. Turn over and cook until the other side is marked, about 3 minutes. (If using an electric grill, keep it open and cook a few minutes longer if necessary.)

Lightly mist four 4-inch springform pans with cooking spray (see Cook Smart). Put a pineapple slice in the bottom of each pan. Divide the couscous evenly among the pans, packing it down firmly using a spoon or the bottom of a measuring cup to form cakes. Refrigerate for at least 1 hour before serving to allow the cakes to firm up. Covered and stored in the refrigerator, the cakes will keep for up to 4 days.

To serve, invert each pan over a plate. Loosen the pan and remove the sides and base. Top with the pomegranate seeds.

Per serving: 278 calories, 7 g protein, 1 g fat (0.1 g sat), 61 g carbs, 148 mg sodium, 25 mg calcium, 5 g fiber

Cook Smart
- This recipe can also be made in a single 8-inch springform pan. Cut the cake into quarters to serve.

While the Girl Scouts don't claim to be the inventors of s'mores, the first known printing of the recipe appeared in the 1920s in their book *Training and Trailing with the Girl Scouts*. This version, which just might be even easier than the campfire original, gets a Mexican twist from ancho chile powder and cinnamon.

MEXICAN S'MORES

Yield: 4 servings

⅔ cup vegan chocolate chips

½ cup chopped vegan marshmallows

¾ teaspoon ancho chile powder

½ teaspoon ground cinnamon

4 (8-inch) flour tortillas

Put the chocolate chips, marshmallows, chile powder, and cinnamon in a medium bowl and stir to combine. Spread the mixture evenly over two of the tortillas. Cover with the remaining tortillas.

Outdoor Grill Method

Preheat an outdoor grill or grill pan to medium heat.

Lightly oil the grill with canola oil. Put the s'mores on the grill and put a cast-iron skillet on top of each to press it. Cook until marked, about 3 minutes. Turn over and cook in the same fashion until the other side is marked, about 2 minutes. Cut each s'more into quarters and serve 2 quarters per person.

Indoor Method

Preheat the oven to 300 degrees F. Line a baking sheet with parchment paper. Preheat a grill pan or electric grill to medium heat.

Assemble the s'mores as directed. Lightly oil the grill pan or electric grill with canola oil. Put one s'more on the grill and, if using an electric grill, close the lid. Cook until marked, about 3 minutes. Transfer the finished s'more to the lined baking sheet, and put it in the oven to keep it hot. Grill the second s'more in the same fashion.

Per serving: 325 calories, 6 g protein, 15 g fat (8 g sat), 51 g carbs, 381 mg sodium, 24 mg calcium, 4 g fiber

The popular combination of marshmallows, nuts, and chocolate that characterizes rocky road candy and ice cream makes an appearance here in a yeasted brownie-like dessert.

ROCKY ROAD FLATBREAD

Yield: 4 servings • Advance prep: The dough must rise for 1½ hours.

1½ cups all-purpose flour, plus more if needed

¼ cup unsweetened cocoa powder

2 tablespoons sugar

½ teaspoon salt

½ cup warm water (about 105 degrees F)

3 tablespoons maple syrup

1 teaspoon active dry yeast

2 tablespoons vegan margarine, melted and cooled slightly

1 teaspoon vanilla extract

½ cup chopped walnuts

⅓ cup coarsely chopped vegan marshmallows

¼ cup vegan chocolate chips

Put the flour, cocoa, sugar, and salt in a medium bowl. Stir to combine.

Put the water, 1 tablespoon of the maple syrup, and the yeast in a small bowl and stir to combine. Set aside for about 5 minutes to proof; the yeast is ready when the mixture bubbles. Stir in the remaining 2 tablespoons of maple syrup and the margarine and vanilla extract. Pour into the flour mixture and stir to combine. If necessary, add up to 2 tablespoons more flour, 1 tablespoon at a time, to make a soft, tacky dough.

Turn the dough out onto a lightly floured work surface and knead until smooth and silky, about 7 minutes. The dough should be soft and moist; if it's sticky, knead in up to 2 tablespoons more flour. Knead in the walnuts until they are evenly distributed. Form the dough into a ball.

Lightly oil a medium bowl with canola oil. Put the dough in the bowl and turn to coat with the oil. Cover with a clean kitchen towel and let rise in a warm place until doubled in size, about 1½ hours (see Cook Smart, page 39).

Outdoor Method

Preheat an outdoor grill to medium-high heat.

Lightly flour a 16-inch piece of parchment paper. Put the dough on the parchment paper and roll it out to a 12-inch round. Lightly oil the grill with canola oil. Carefully transfer the dough to the grill by inverting it onto the grill and peeling off the parchment paper. Close the lid. Cook until the bottom is marked, about 3 minutes. Turn over and sprinkle the marshmallows and chocolate chips evenly over the top. Close the lid and cook until the marshmallows are toasted and the chocolate chips are melted, about 4 minutes.

Indoor Method

Preheat the oven to 400 degrees F. Lightly oil a baking sheet with canola oil.

Roll out the dough as directed and transfer it to the prepared baking sheet. Bake for about 8 minutes, until a toothpick inserted in the center comes out clean. Sprinkle the marshmallows and chocolate chips evenly over the top and bake until the marshmallows are toasted and the chocolate chips are melted, about 3 minutes.

Per serving: 465 calories, 11 g protein, 21 g fat (7 g sat), 67 g carbs, 195 mg sodium, 59 mg calcium, 7 g fiber

This dessert, which is somewhat like a coffee cake and somewhat like cinnamon rolls, is sure to be greeted with smiles any time of day or night. Why not make it for dessert and enjoy the leftovers for breakfast? Seasoned with cinnamon and ginger, studded with raisins, and drizzled with a cream cheese glaze, it's a treat for both the eyes and the taste buds.

CINNAMON SWIRL

Yield: One 8-inch roll, 6 servings • *Advance prep: The dough must rise for 2¼ hours.*

Roll

1¾ cups all-purpose flour, plus more
   if needed

¼ cup raisins

1 teaspoon ground ginger

½ teaspoon salt

½ cup warm water (about
   105 degrees F), plus more
   if needed

3 tablespoons maple syrup

1 teaspoon active dry yeast

2 tablespoons canola oil

2 tablespoons vegan margarine, at
   room temperature

⅓ cup light brown sugar, firmly
   packed

1 teaspoon ground cinnamon

To make the roll, put the flour, raisins, ginger, and salt in a medium bowl and stir to combine.

Put the water, 1 tablespoon of the maple syrup, and the yeast in a small bowl and stir to combine. Set aside for about 5 minutes for the yeast to proof; the yeast is ready when the mixture bubbles. Stir in the remaining 2 tablespoons of maple syrup and the oil. Pour into the flour mixture and stir to combine. If necessary, add up to 1 more tablespoon of water or flour, 1 teaspoon at a time, until the dough comes together and is firm enough to knead.

Turn the dough out onto a lightly floured work surface and knead until smooth and silky, about 8 minutes. Form the dough into a ball.

Lightly oil a medium bowl with canola oil. Put the dough in the bowl and turn to coat with the oil. Cover with a clean kitchen towel and let rise in a warm place until doubled in size, about 1½ hours (see Cook Smart, page 39).

Melt 1 tablespoon of the margarine in an 8-inch cast-iron skillet over low heat. Swirl the margarine to coat the bottom of the skillet. Remove from the heat.

Put the brown sugar and cinnamon in a small bowl and stir to combine.

Transfer the dough to a lightly floured work surface and roll it out to a 14 x 12-inch rectangle. Spread the remaining tablespoon of margarine evenly over the dough, then sprinkle the brown sugar mixture evenly over the margarine. Roll up tightly to form a log. Pat and roll the finished log with your hands, gently stretching it until it is 16 to 18 inches long. Put one end of the log in the center

Glaze

¾ cup confectioners' sugar

2 tablespoons vegan cream cheese

1 to 2 teaspoons plain soy milk

½ teaspoon vanilla extract

Pinch salt

of the skillet and wind the log into a spiral. Cover with the towel and let rise in a warm place until doubled in size, about 45 minutes.

To make the glaze, put the confectioners' sugar, vegan cream cheese, 1 teaspoon of the soy milk, and the vanilla extract and salt in a medium bowl. Beat until smooth with an electric mixer. If necessary, add the remaining teaspoon of soy milk to make a thick glaze that can be drizzled.

Outdoor Method

Put a large cast-iron skillet upside down on an outdoor grill to slightly elevate the skillet containing the roll. Preheat the grill to medium heat.

Put the skillet containing the roll on top of the inverted skillet. Close the grill and cook for 7 to 8 minutes. Check to see if the top is getting too brown; if it is, cover the skillet loosely with foil. Cook until the bottom is golden, 3 to 5 minutes longer. Invert onto a plate and drizzle with the glaze.

Indoor Method

Preheat the oven to 375 degrees F. Bake the roll for 15 minutes. Check to see if the top is getting too brown; if it is, cover the skillet loosely with foil. Bake until the bottom is golden, 5 to 7 minutes longer. Invert onto a plate and drizzle with the glaze.

Per serving: 356 calories, 5 g protein, 10 g fat (2 g sat), 65 g carbs, 270 mg sodium, 17 mg calcium, 2 g fiber

Chapter 7

Remarkable Rubs, Marinades, and Sauces

This seasoning is quick, easy, and wonderful on seitan, tofu, and tempeh. It's also a must for Seitan and Potato Salad with Horseradish Dressing (page 78).

ALL-PURPOSE DRY RUB

Yield: ²/₃ cup

4 tablespoons paprika

2 tablespoons ground cumin

2 tablespoons onion powder

1 tablespoon ground pepper

½ tablespoon salt

Put all the ingredients in a small bowl and stir to combine. Stored in a tightly closed jar or ziplock bag at room temperature, the rub will keep for 6 months.

Per 1 teaspoon: 6 calories, 0 g protein, 0.2 g fat (0 g sat), 1 g carbs, 37 mg sodium, 8 mg calcium, 0 g fiber

Cook Smart

- If you'd like to experiment with this as a wet rub, add 2 teaspoons of olive oil per tablespoon of dry rub.

Some cookbooks offer recipes for spice blends that yield a huge amount. I often scale them back, but when I find one I really like and use frequently, I make a big batch. You'll want to keep this rub on hand for Seitan Potato Sticks (page 99), Seitan Ribz (page 94), and Barbecue Sauce in a Flash (page 165).

BARBECUE RUB

Yield: 1 cup

4 tablespoons dry mustard

4 tablespoons onion powder

4 tablespoons smoked paprika

2 tablespoons garlic powder

1 tablespoon ground cumin

1 tablespoon ground pepper

Put all the ingredients in a small bowl and stir to combine. Stored in a tightly closed jar or ziplock bag at room temperature, the rub will keep for 6 months.

Per 1 teaspoon: 8 calories, 0 g protein, 0.3 g fat (0.1 g sat), 2 g carbs, 1 mg sodium, 6 mg calcium, 1 g fiber

This blend of harissa spices can be used as a dry rub for tofu, tempeh, or seitan before cooking for instant flavor. For a wet rub, mix equal parts of the spice blend with olive oil. Harissa is traditionally customized to a family's taste, so feel free to adjust the amount of cayenne—or any of the ingredients, for that matter.

HARISSA DRY MIX

Yield: ½ cup

2 tablespoons chili powder

4 teaspoons ground coriander

4 teaspoons smoked paprika

2 teaspoons garlic powder

2 teaspoons salt

1½ teaspoons ground cayenne

1 teaspoon ground cardamom

1 teaspoon ground cumin

½ teaspoon ground cloves

½ teaspoon ground pepper

Put all the ingredients in a small bowl and stir to combine. Stored in a tightly closed jar or ziplock bag at room temperature, the spice mixture will keep for 6 months.

Per 1 teaspoon: 6 calories, 0 g protein, 0.3 g fat (0 g sat), 1 g carbs, 197 mg sodium, 5 mg calcium, 6 g fiber

North African harissa paste is a piquant, flavorful blend of chiles and spices. It's typically used as a flavoring for stews or couscous but is very versatile and enhances many other dishes. Traditionally, the paste is made at home to each family's liking. In keeping with that tradition, I encourage you to think of this recipe as a blueprint, customizing it to your taste.

HARISSA PASTE

Yield: ¾ cup

6 dried New Mexico chiles, stemmed and seeded

1 dried ancho chile, stemmed and seeded

½ roasted red bell pepper (see page 14)

¼ cup moist-packed sun-dried tomatoes

Juice from ½ lemon

2 tablespoons extra-virgin olive oil

1 tablespoon red wine vinegar

3 cloves garlic, minced

½ teaspoon ground caraway seeds

½ teaspoon red pepper flakes

¼ teaspoon ground pepper

Put the dried chiles in a heatproof bowl. Pour about 4 cups of boiling water over them and put a small plate on top of the peppers to keep them submerged. Let rest for 30 minutes to rehydrate.

Drain the chiles, discarding the liquid, and transfer to a food processor or blender. Add the bell pepper, sun-dried tomatoes, lemon juice, oil, vinegar, garlic, caraway seeds, red pepper flakes, and pepper and process until smooth. Stored in a covered container in the refrigerator, the paste will keep for 1 month.

Per 1 teaspoon: 12 calories, 0 g protein, 1 g fat (0.1 g sat), 1 g carbs, 2 mg sodium, 14 mg calcium, 0 g fiber

Cook Smart

- If you'd prefer to buy harissa paste rather than make your own, look for it at African markets or in the international aisle of well-stocked supermarkets. Because the heat levels of different brands vary, be sure to add it to recipes to taste.

If you're looking for instant smoke flavor using only a minimal amount of liquid smoke, this is the recipe for you. It includes Lapsang souchong tea, which has a complex flavor created by smoking the tea leaves over burning pinewood. Here, it's combined with smoky spices in a concoction that will make any recipe pop with campfire flavor. Look for Lapsang souchong tea in well-stocked grocery stores, especially those that sell loose teas in tins and bulk teas.

SMOKE BOOSTER

Yield: ½ cup

½ cup boiling water

1 teaspoon Lapsang souchong tea leaves

1 teaspoon liquid smoke

½ teaspoon smoked paprika

¼ teaspoon onion powder

¼ teaspoon salt

¼ teaspoon molasses

⅛ teaspoon ground cumin

Pinch ground pepper

Pour the water over the tea leaves and let steep for 4 minutes. Strain into a small jar and discard the tea leaves. Add the liquid smoke, paprika, onion powder, salt, molasses, cumin, and pepper. Seal the jar tightly and shake vigorously to combine. Stored in the sealed jar in the refrigerator, the mixture will keep for 1 week.

Per 1 tablespoon: 2 calories, 0 g protein, 0 g fat (0 g sat), 0 g carbs, 73 mg sodium, 1 mg calcium, 0 g fiber

With its roots in Asian cuisine, this lively marinade combines ginger, garlic, and other seasonings to create delectably bold flavors that bring out the best in whatever you choose to use with it. Try it in Teppanyaki Seitan Wraps (page 54) or Seitan and Cucumber Minis (page 43). It also works well as a marinade for tofu or portobello mushrooms and is a superlative sauce for stir-fries.

SWEET-AND-SPICY MARINADE

Yield: 1 1/2 cups

2 cups salt-free vegetable broth

2 tablespoons light brown sugar

2 tablespoons reduced-sodium tamari

1 tablespoon seasoned rice vinegar

1 (1-inch) piece fresh ginger, coarsely chopped

3 cloves garlic, cut in half

1 scallion, cut into 2-inch pieces

3 star anise pods (see Cook Smart)

1 teaspoon hot chile oil

1 teaspoon black peppercorns

Put all the ingredients in a medium saucepan and stir to combine. Bring to a boil over medium-high heat. Decrease the heat to low and simmer uncovered, stirring occasionally, for 30 minutes. Strain the marinade and discard the solids. Stored in a covered container in the refrigerator, the marinade will keep for 1 week.

Per 1/4 cup: 41 calories, 1 g protein, 1 g fat (0 g sat), 7 g carbs, 278 mg sodium, 6 mg calcium, 0 g fiber

Cook Smart

• Although the plants that produce star anise and regular anise are unrelated, star anise pods and anise seeds both contain anethole, which gives them their distinctive flavor. However, star anise is a bit more bitter. Look for it in Asian markets and spice shops. You may also find it in the spice section at well-stocked grocery stores.

Habanero chiles are small, round, and fiery and turn a beautiful shade of orange when ripe. If they aren't available, substitute Scotch bonnet peppers, which are similar in size, shape, texture, and heat level.

HABANERO MARINADE

Yield: 1 ½ cups

1 cup salt-free vegetable broth

½ cup coarsely chopped onion

½ cup cider vinegar

4 habanero chiles, stemmed and seeded (see Cook Smart)

¼ cup sugar

2 tablespoons reduced-sodium tamari

1 tablespoon canola oil

1 tablespoon no-salt-added tomato paste

2 cloves garlic, sliced

¼ teaspoon ground pepper

Put all the ingredients in a small saucepan and stir to combine. Bring to a boil over medium-high heat. Decrease the heat to low and simmer uncovered, stirring occasionally, for 15 minutes. Strain the marinade and discard the solids. Stored in a covered container in the refrigerator, the marinade will keep for 1 week.

Per ¼ cup: 113 calories, 1 g protein, 3 g fat (0.1 g sat), 21 g carbs, 263 mg sodium, 6 mg calcium, 1 g fiber

Cook Smart

• Habanero chiles are very hot. Be sure to wear gloves when handling them, and don't touch your eyes or other sensitive areas afterward.

It's easier to buy a bottle of ketchup at the store, but this homemade version, which is fairly effortless to prepare, will make any cookout more memorable. Surprisingly, even those who aren't big fans of ketchup love this recipe. For a spicier condiment, choose fire-roasted tomatoes that have chiles added.

SPICED KETCHUP

Yield: 2 cups

1 teaspoon olive oil

¼ cup chopped red onion

½ teaspoon salt, plus more if desired

¼ teaspoon ground pepper, plus more if desired

1 (15-ounce) can fire-roasted crushed tomatoes

1 (6-ounce) can no-salt-added tomato paste

3 tablespoons cider vinegar

1 tablespoon molasses

2 teaspoons minced chipotle chiles in adobo sauce, plus more if desired

Heat the oil in a medium saucepan over medium heat. Add the onion, salt, and pepper and cook, stirring occasionally, until fragrant, about 3 minutes. Stir in the tomatoes, tomato paste, vinegar, molasses, and chiles. Decrease the heat to low and simmer uncovered, stirring occasionally, for 15 minutes.

Let cool slightly. Transfer to a blender and process until smooth. Stored in a covered container in the refrigerator, the ketchup will keep for 1 month.

Per 2 tablespoons: 24 calories, 0 g protein, 1 g fat (0.1 g sat), 3 g carbs, 131 mg sodium, 14 mg calcium, 0 g fiber

This homemade barbecue sauce tastes better than store-bought versions and comes together in about fifteen minutes. It has a sweet undertone from the dark brown sugar, brightness from the rice vinegar, and complex flavor from the spices in the Barbecue Rub.

BARBECUE SAUCE IN A FLASH

Yield: 2 cups • Advance prep: Make Barbecue Rub (page 158).

1½ cups ketchup

½ cup minced onion

½ cup dark brown sugar, lightly packed

½ cup seasoned rice vinegar

4 cloves garlic, minced

2 teaspoons Barbecue Rub (page 158)

½ teaspoon ground cayenne

¼ teaspoon ground pepper

Put all the ingredients in a medium saucepan and stir to combine. Bring to a boil over medium-high heat. Decrease the heat to low and simmer uncovered, stirring occasionally, for 15 minutes.

Per 2 tablespoons: 65 calories, 1 g protein, 0 g fat (0 g sat), 17 g carbs, 330 mg sodium, 2 mg calcium, 0 g fiber

BLENDED BARBECUE SAUCE: For a completely smooth sauce (without any texture from the onions), let the sauce cool a bit after cooking. Then put it in a blender and process until smooth.

Essential for Teriyaki Portobello Burgers (page 64) and Ramen-Broccoli Salad with Grilled Portobellos (page 74), this sauce can also be used to dress up seitan, tofu, tempeh, or vegetables. Add a little to fried rice or cold Asian noodle salads for extra zing. Of course, it's a natural in stir-fries.

TERIYAKI SAUCE

Yield: 1 ½ cups

1 teaspoon toasted sesame oil

2 tablespoons minced scallion

2 cloves garlic, minced

1 teaspoon grated fresh ginger

1½ cups salt-free vegetable broth

¼ cup mirin

¼ cup reduced-sodium tamari

2 tablespoons agave nectar

2 teaspoons molasses

2 tablespoons cornstarch

Heat the oil in a medium saucepan over medium heat. Add the scallion, garlic, and ginger and cook, stirring occasionally, until fragrant, about 2 minutes. Stir in 1 cup of the broth and the mirin, tamari, agave nectar, and molasses. Increase the heat to medium-high and bring to a boil. Decrease the heat to low and simmer uncovered, stirring occasionally, until about one-quarter of the liquid has evaporated, about 10 minutes.

Put the remaining ½ cup of broth in a small bowl. Add the cornstarch and whisk to form a slurry. Slowly pour the slurry into the saucepan while whisking constantly. Cook, whisking constantly, until thickened, about 3 minutes. Stored in a covered container in the refrigerator, the sauce will keep for 1 week.

Per 2 tablespoons: 46 calories, 1 g protein, 0.4 g fat (0 g sat), 9 g carbs, 237 mg sodium, 4 mg calcium, 0 g fiber

Warning! If you make this five-alarm hot sauce indoors, it will create a pungent peppery smoke, so open the windows if possible. Spicy-food fans will probably have lots of ideas about how to use this condiment. But just in case, here are a few suggestions to get you started: spread it sparingly on corn on the cob, mix it with melted vegan margarine to coat popcorn, or add it to bean dishes, Bloody Marys, cooked grains, gravies, macaroni salad, or potato salad.

HABANERO LAVA

Yield: ½ cup

10 habanero peppers, stemmed and seeded (see Cook Smart, page 163)

2 teaspoons canola oil

2 tablespoons chopped grilled onion (see page 14)

1 tablespoon agave nectar

1 tablespoon red wine vinegar

½ teaspoon salt

Preheat a grill, grill pan, or electric grill to medium-high heat.

Put the peppers in a bowl. Drizzle with the oil and toss until the peppers are evenly coated. Put the peppers on the grill and cook, turning occasionally, until blackened in spots and soft, about 7 minutes. (If using an electric grill, keep it open and cook a few minutes longer if necessary.)

Put the peppers in a blender. Add the onion, agave nectar, vinegar, and salt and process until smooth. Stored in a covered container in the refrigerator, the sauce will keep for 1 month.

Per 1 teaspoon: 14 calories, 0 g protein, 0.4 g fat (0 g sat), 2 g carbs, 49 mg sodium, 0 mg calcium, 0 g fiber

Cook Smart

• The habanero plant is a perennial that thrives in hot weather. If you love spicy food and live in a warm climate, try growing one as a container plant.

This zesty sauce, which is used in Chimichurri Wraps (page 52), is also terrific over grilled tofu, tempeh, or vegetables. You'll find endless uses for it: Try adding a tablespoon of the sauce to a soup to give it some oomph, or to potato salad, macaroni salad, or coleslaw for a spicier side dish. It's especially at home with Latin American cuisines, so stir a bit into beans or a burrito filling to take the flavor up a notch.

RED-HOT CHIMICHURRI SAUCE

Yield: 1 cup

1 cup coarsely chopped roasted red bell peppers (see page 14)

2 tablespoons red wine vinegar

1 chipotle chile in adobo sauce, chopped (see Cook Smart)

2 cloves garlic, minced

1 teaspoon ground cumin

½ teaspoon agave nectar

½ teaspoon ground coriander

½ teaspoon dried oregano

½ teaspoon smoked paprika

¼ teaspoon salt

Pinch ground pepper

Put all the ingredients in a small blender or food processor and process until smooth. Stored in a covered container in the refrigerator, the sauce will keep for 1 week. Stir it before each use.

Per 1 tablespoon: 8 calories, 0 g protein, 0.3 g fat (0 g sat), 1 g carbs, 112 mg sodium, 2 mg calcium, 0 g fiber

Cook Smart

- If you have a high threshold for heat, use two chipotle chiles instead of just one, to ramp up the spice level.

This sauce is sensational over grilled seitan or vegetables, on potatoes, or as a dip for fried foods. It also peps up sandwiches when used as a spread.

TANGY DIJON SAUCE

Yield: ¹/₂ cup

¹/₃ cup Dijon mustard

¼ cup salt-free vegetable broth

2 tablespoons maple syrup

1 tablespoon hot sauce

½ teaspoon garlic powder

½ teaspoon onion powder

¼ teaspoon red pepper flakes

¹/₈ teaspoon ground pepper

Salt (optional)

Put the mustard, broth, maple syrup, hot sauce, garlic powder, onion powder, red pepper flakes, and pepper in a small saucepan and stir to combine. Bring to a boil over medium-high heat. Decrease the heat to low and simmer uncovered, stirring occasionally, for 5 minutes to allow the flavors to meld. Season with salt to taste if desired. Stored in a covered container in the refrigerator, the sauce will keep for 1 week.

Per tablespoon: 26 calories, 0 g protein, 1 g fat (0 g sat), 4 g carbs, 444 mg sodium, 3 mg calcium, 0 g fiber

Cook Smart

• To reheat the sauce, warm it gently over medium-low heat until steaming, about 4 minutes. Add a bit of broth if the sauce is too thick.

This lively sauce has undercurrents of ginger and garam masala. Try it on any protein, such as grilled Classic Cutlets (page 91) or tempeh, or, my favorite way, as a marinade and topping for Fruited Tofu Skewers (page 115).

SAVORY APRICOT SAUCE

Yield: 1 cup

1 pound fresh apricots, pitted and diced (see Cook Smart)

¼ cup minced onion

¼ cup minced red bell pepper

1 tablespoon agave nectar

1 tablespoon white balsamic vinegar

1 teaspoon grated fresh ginger

½ teaspoon hot chile oil

¼ teaspoon garam masala

¼ teaspoon ground white pepper

¼ teaspoon salt

Put all the ingredients in a medium saucepan and stir to combine. Bring to a boil over medium-high heat. Decrease the heat to low and simmer uncovered, stirring frequently, until the apricots are broken down and the sauce is thick, about 30 minutes. Stored in a covered container in the refrigerator, the sauce will keep for 1 week.

Per 2 tablespoons: 43 calories, 1 g protein, 0.4 g fat (0 g sat), 10 g carbs, 72 mg sodium, 2 mg calcium, 1 g fiber

Cook Smart
- If fresh apricots aren't available, substitute 1 (15-ounce) can unsweetened apricots. Drain them before using.
- If you prefer a thinner sauce, stir in 1 to 2 tablespoons of salt-free vegetable broth when you remove the sauce from the heat.

Pair this vibrant red sauce, which takes only a few moments to prepare, with any grilled protein or vegetable. Or try it over pasta or baked potatoes. It's got the perfect balance of sweet and heat.

BELL PEPPER AND SUN-DRIED TOMATO SAUCE

Yield: 1½ cups • Advance prep: Soak the cashews for 1 hour.

1 cup chopped roasted red bell peppers (see page 14)

4 moist-packed sun-dried tomato halves

¼ cup cashews, soaked in cold water for 1 hour and drained

Juice from ½ lemon

2 tablespoons vegan mayonnaise

1 tablespoon white wine vinegar

1 tablespoon reduced-sodium tamari

1 teaspoon harissa paste, homemade (page 160) or store-bought

1 clove garlic, minced

½ teaspoon agave nectar or sugar

½ teaspoon salt

¼ teaspoon ground pepper

1 to 3 tablespoons salt-free vegetable broth

Put the bell pepper, sun-dried tomatoes, cashews, lemon juice, vegan mayonnaise, vinegar, tamari, harissa paste, garlic, agave nectar, salt, and pepper in a blender or food processor and process until smooth. With the motor running, add the broth through the cap opening in the lid, 1 tablespoon at a time, until the sauce has the desired consistency.

This sauce may be served hot or at room temperature. To heat, transfer to a medium saucepan over medium-low heat. Cook uncovered, stirring occasionally, until steaming, about 4 minutes. Stored in a covered container in the refrigerator, the sauce will keep for 1 week.

Per ¼ cup: 79 calories, 2 g protein, 5 g fat (1 g sat), 5 g carbs, 505 mg sodium, 6 mg calcium, 0 g fiber

This sauce packs a punch when served over any grilled protein and shines on Tomato-Arugula Flatbread (page 35). It's also delicious on portobello burgers and other sandwiches.

CREAMY HORSERADISH SAUCE

Yield: ¹/₂ cup

6 tablespoons vegan mayonnaise

1 tablespoon vegan prepared horseradish

1 tablespoon cider vinegar

1½ teaspoons Dijon mustard

Pinch salt

Pinch ground pepper

Put all the ingredients in a small bowl and stir to combine. Stored in a covered container in the refrigerator, the sauce will keep for 3 days.

Per 1 tablespoon: 70 calories, 0 g protein, 7 g fat (1 g sat), 0 g carbs, 160 mg sodium, 1 mg calcium, 0 g fiber

Three little ingredients never tasted so big. This spicy sauce draws out the flavors of Tunisian Skewers with Lemon-Kissed Couscous (page 104). Also try it over any grilled tofu dish or cooked grain.

CREAMY HARISSA SAUCE

Yield: ¹/₂ cup • Advance prep: Soak the cashews for 1 hour.

½ cup salt-free vegetable broth

⅓ cup cashews, soaked in cold water for 1 hour and drained

1 tablespoon harissa paste, homemade (page 160) or store-bought, plus more if desired

Put the broth, cashews, and 1 tablespoon of the harissa paste in a small blender and process until completely smooth. Taste and add up to 1 more tablespoon of harissa paste if desired. Stored in a covered container in the refrigerator, the sauce will keep for 3 days.

Per 2 tablespoons: 66 calories, 2 g protein, 5 g fat (0.8 g sat), 4 g carbs, 40 mg sodium, 9 mg calcium, 0 g fiber

This lively green sauce is featured as a topping on Red Bell Pepper Gazpacho (page 48) and Quinoa-Stuffed Poblanos (page 100), but you're sure to find many other uses for it. Try it on burritos, burgers, or sandwiches, or use it to make a Mexican potato salad. Because avocados turn brown when exposed to air, it's best to serve this sauce soon after you make it.

AVOCADO SAUCE

Yield: ¾ cup

1 large avocado, cut into chunks

⅔ cup fresh cilantro leaves, lightly packed

½ cup minced scallions

½ cup water

Juice from 1 lime

1 jalapeño chile, seeded and chopped

1 tablespoon seasoned rice vinegar

2 cloves garlic, minced

½ teaspoon salt

¼ teaspoon ground pepper

Put all the ingredients in a blender and process until smooth and creamy. Serve immediately or cover tightly and refrigerate for up to 2 hours before serving.

Per 1 tablespoon: 25 calories, 0 g protein, 2 g fat (0.3 g sat), 2 g carbs, 116 mg sodium, 6 mg calcium, 1 g fiber

This creamy, herb-flecked sauce can be used in many ways. Try it on Buffalo Pizza (page 110) or as a dipping sauce for Seitan Ribz (page 94). It's also a lovely salad dressing or sandwich spread.

CASHEW RANCH SAUCE

Yield: ¾ cup

¾ cup cashews

5 tablespoons unsweetened soy milk

¼ cup white wine vinegar

2 tablespoons minced onion

1 tablespoon nutritional yeast flakes

1 clove garlic, minced

¼ teaspoon celery salt

¼ teaspoon ground white pepper

1 tablespoon minced fresh parsley, or 1 teaspoon dried

½ teaspoon minced fresh thyme, or ⅛ teaspoon dried

Put the cashews in a blender and process until powdered. Add the soy milk, vinegar, onion, nutritional yeast, garlic, celery salt, and white pepper and process until completely smooth. Transfer to a small bowl and stir in the parsley and thyme. Stored in a covered container in the refrigerator, the sauce will keep for 1 week.

Per 1 tablespoon: 44 calories, 2 g protein, 3 g fat (1 g sat), 3 g carbs, 25 mg sodium, 14 mg calcium, 0 g fiber

Essential for Panzanella with Tempeh (page 77), this dressing can also be used as a marinade for tofu, tempeh, or portobello mushrooms. Of course, it's a wonderful salad dressing too.

ITALIAN DRESSING

Yield: ³/₄ cup

¼ cup red wine vinegar

2 tablespoons freshly squeezed lemon juice

1 tablespoon capers

1 tablespoon caper brine

2 cloves garlic, minced

1 teaspoon maple syrup

1 teaspoon Dijon mustard

½ teaspoon ground pepper

⅛ teaspoon salt

3 tablespoons extra-virgin olive oil

Put the vinegar, lemon juice, capers, caper brine, garlic, maple syrup, mustard, pepper, and salt in a blender and process until smooth. With the motor running, slowly add the oil through the cap opening in the lid and process until completely smooth and well blended. Stored in a covered container in the refrigerator, the dressing will keep for 1 week.

Per 2 tablespoons: 67 calories, 10 g protein, 7 g fat (1 g sat), 2 g carbs, 107 mg sodium, 3 mg calcium, 0 g fiber

This salad dressing is sure to become a favorite in your home, especially for salads featuring grilled vegetables. The unbeatable combination of sun-dried tomatoes and roasted garlic is even better with the addition of capers and Mediterranean herbs. It has so many flavors to excite the palate that no one will believe it's virtually fat-free.

ROASTED GARLIC DRESSING

Yield: ³/₄ cup • Advance prep: Make Roasted Garlic (page 20).

½ cup salt-free vegetable broth

3 tablespoons cider vinegar

Juice from ½ lemon

2 tablespoons minced moist-packed sun-dried tomatoes

6 cloves Roasted Garlic (page 20)

2 teaspoons dried basil

1 teaspoon capers

1 teaspoon caper brine

½ teaspoon dried marjoram

½ teaspoon dried thyme

½ teaspoon ground pepper

Salt (optional)

Put the broth, vinegar, lemon juice, sun-dried tomatoes, garlic, basil, capers, brine, marjoram, thyme, and pepper in a blender and process until smooth. Season with salt to taste if desired. Stored in a covered container in the refrigerator, the dressing will keep for 1 week.

Per 2 tablespoons: 13 calories, 0 g protein, 1 g fat (0.2 g sat), 2 g carbs, 77 mg sodium, 12 mg calcium, 0 g fiber

This dressing adds a colorful accent to any grilled vegetable, especially asparagus or cauliflower. You might also try it in a potato or macaroni salad. Tangy, with a hint of onion and heat, it's very versatile.

RUSSIAN DRESSING WITH A KICK

Yield: ³/₄ cup • Advance prep: Soak the cashews for 1 hour.

½ cup cashews, soaked in cold water for 1 hour and drained

¼ cup unsweetened soy milk

2 tablespoons ketchup

2 tablespoons minced onion

2 tablespoons red wine vinegar

2 teaspoons capers

1 teaspoon olive oil

⅛ teaspoon ground pepper

Hot sauce

Put cashews, soy milk, ketchup, onion, vinegar, capers, oil, and pepper in a small blender or food processor and process until completely smooth. Season with hot sauce to taste. Stored in a covered container in the refrigerator, the dressing will keep for 1 week.

Per 2 tablespoons: 71 calories, 2 g protein, 5 g fat (1 g sat), 5 g carbs, 78 mg sodium, 21 mg calcium, 1 g fiber

This creamy, zingy dressing has a rich, full taste accented with smoky flavor, yet it has no added oil. Try it as a dipping sauce for grilled skewers or drizzled over other grilled proteins for a savory and satisfying finishing touch.

SCALLION-TAHINI DRESSING

Yield: 2 1/2 cups

10 scallions

1 cup salt-free vegetable broth

⅓ cup seasoned rice vinegar

¼ cup tahini

Juice from ½ lime

1 teaspoon red pepper flakes

1 teaspoon umeboshi plum paste (see Cook Smart)

½ teaspoon agave nectar

¼ teaspoon salt

Pinch ground pepper

Preheat a grill, grill pan, or electric grill to medium-high heat.

Lightly oil the grill with canola oil. Put the scallions on the grill and cook until marked, about 4 minutes. Turn over and cook until the other side is marked, about 2 minutes. (If using an electric grill, keep it open and cook a few minutes longer if necessary.)

When the scallions are cool enough to handle, trim and chop them. Transfer to a blender. Add the broth, vinegar, tahini, lime juice, red pepper flakes, umeboshi plum paste, agave nectar, salt, and pepper and process until smooth. Stored in a covered container in the refrigerator, the dressing will keep for 4 days.

Per 2 tablespoons: 29 calories, 1 g protein, 2 g fat (0.3 g sat), 3 g carbs, 109 mg sodium, 9 mg calcium, 0 g fiber

Cook Smart

• Umeboshi plum paste, a Japanese condiment, is made by mashing pickled umeboshi plums. It's a reddish concentrate with an intense salty, tangy taste. Look for it in the Asian section of well-stocked supermarkets.

GLOSSARY

Agave nectar. Agave nectar is a syrupy liquid sweetener produced from the sap of the agave plant, a type of succulent that grows in Mexico and South Africa.

Chickpea flour. Made from ground dried chickpeas, chickpea flour is higher in protein than most flours and contains no gluten. It's used in many different cuisines but is perhaps best known for its role in Indian food. Look for chickpea flour in Indian grocery stores, the natural food section of well-stocked supermarkets, or at natural food stores.

Five-spice powder. So named because it's a blend of five spices—cinnamon, cloves, fennel, Sichuan peppercorns, and star anise—five-spice powder is a popular Chinese seasoning.

Garam masala. Garam masala is a potent Indian spice blend composed of ingredients that vary from region to region. It can have many ingredients, some of which may be spicy.

Harissa paste: I offer a recipe for harissa paste, a spicy condiment that is popular in North African cuisine, on page 160. However, if you'd prefer to buy harissa paste rather than make your own, look for it at African markets or in the spice or international aisle of well-stocked supermarkets. Because the heat levels of different brands vary, be sure to add it to recipes to taste.

Herbes de Provence. Hailing from the Provence region of France, herbes de Provence is a dried blend that includes basil, fennel, rosemary, thyme, and other herbs.

Liquid smoke. A concentrated flavoring, liquid smoke should be used only sparingly. It's made by passing various types of smoke, most often hickory smoke, through water. It adds a rich, smoky flavor to food.

Mirin. A slightly sweet, strongly flavored rice wine from Japan, mirin is available at natural food stores and well-stocked supermarkets. In a pinch, dry sherry may be substituted.

Miso. A fermented bean paste used in Japanese cooking, miso is best known for its role in miso soup. This thick, salty, concentrated seasoning is packed with flavor. Lighter-colored miso is mild and slightly sweet, while darker miso tends to be more hearty and salty. Miso can be stored in the refrigerator for up to a year after purchase.

Nutritional yeast. Sold as powder or flakes, nutritional yeast enhances both flavor and nutrition. Flakes are preferable for the recipes in this book. With its cheesy flavor, nutritional yeast adds richness to soups, sauces, dressings, and main dishes. Store nutritional yeast in a sealed container at room temperature, away from direct heat and light.

Seitan. Seitan is a concentrated protein made from wheat gluten. It has a dense, meaty texture and is ideal for grilling. Store seitan in the refrigerator or freezer. Freezing doesn't affect its taste or texture.

Sriracha sauce. Originally from Thailand, sriracha sauce is made from hot chiles, vinegar, garlic, sugar, and salt. Sometimes called rooster sauce, it's a popular condiment in Asian cooking and adds a distinctive flavor to marinades, soups, and other dishes.

Tamari. A type of Japanese soy sauce, tamari is naturally fermented and has a rich, complex flavor. There are many varieties available, including a reduced-sodium option, which I prefer and call for in the recipes in this book.

Tempeh. Tempeh is made from hulled and partially cooked soybeans that are formed into a cake and fermented. Tempeh is a good protein source and is rich in vitamins and fiber. Store tempeh in the refrigerator or freezer.

Tofu. Made from soy milk that's coagulated and pressed into blocks, tofu absorbs flavors well. Chinese-style tofu, also called regular tofu, is the main type used in this book. It's available in soft, firm, and extra-firm varieties. The latter is dense enough that it holds together and grills well, so that's the variety called for in most of the recipes in this book. Always store tofu in the refrigerator.

Ume plum vinegar. Ume plum vinegar is a salty and sour Japanese seasoning. Use it sparingly to add a sharp, salty flavor to any dish that needs a lift. If you do so, you'll probably want to decrease the amount of salt in the recipe. Seasoned rice vinegar is an acceptable alternative, though it doesn't have the same distinctive flavor.

Vital wheat gluten. Derived from wheat flour, vital wheat gluten is used by bakers to enhance the elasticity of bread dough and improve the rise of yeasted baked goods. It is also essential for making seitan, as in the recipes for Seitan Roasts (page 90) and Classic Cutlets (page 91).

White balsamic vinegar. White balsamic vinegar is slightly less sweet and cloying than regular balsamic vinegar. Because of its pale color, it's also more aesthetically pleasing in some recipes. If you don't have white balsamic vinegar on hand, you can substitute cider vinegar.

INDEX

Book Publishing Co.

books that educate, inspire, and empower

To find your favorite vegetarian and soyfood products online, visit:

www.healthy-eating.com

Artisan Vegan Cheese
Miyoko Schinner
978-1-57067-283-5 $19.95

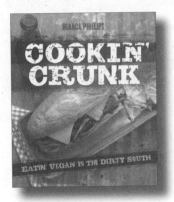

Cookin' Crunk
Bianca Phillips
978-1-57067-268-2 $19.95

The New Enlightened Eating
Caroline Marie Dupont
978-0-92047-083-1 $19.95

The 4 Ingredient Vegan
*Maribeth Abrams, with
Anne Dinshah*
978-1-57067-232-3 $14.95

Cooking Vegan
*Vesanto Melina, MS, RD,
Joseph Forest*
978-1-57067-267-5 $19.95

Local Bounty
Devra Gartenstein
978-1-57067-219-4 $17.95

Purchase these health titles and cookbooks from your local bookstore or natural food store,
or you can buy them directly from:

Book Publishing Company • P.O. Box 99 • Summertown, TN 38483 • 1-800-695-2241

Please include $3.95 per book for shipping and handling.

Harissa Seitan Burgers, p. 68